MEGAN HUNTER & AND

THE
HIGH-CONFLICT
CO-PARENTING
SURVIVAL GUIDE

UNHOOKED BOOKS
An Imprint of High-Conflict Institute Press
Scottsdale, Arizona

PUBLISHER'S NOTE

This publication is designed to provide accurate and authoritative information about the subject matters covered. It is sold with the understanding that neither the authors nor the publisher are rendering mental health, medical, legal or other professional services, either directly or indirectly. If expert assistance, legal, counseling, medical or other assistance is needed, the services of a competent professional should be sought. Neither the authors nor the publisher shall be liable or responsible for any loss or damage allegedly arising as a consequence of your use or application of any information or suggestions in this book.

Copyright © 2019 by Megan Hunter and Andrea Larochelle
Unhooked Books, Llc
7701 E. Indian School Rd., Ste. F
Scottsdale, Az 85251

www.unhookedbooks.com

ISBN: 978-1-936268-30-6
eISBN: 978-1-936268-00-0

Library of Congress Control Number: 2018953503

Book design by Julian Leon, themissive.com
Printed in the United States of America

CONTENTS

A NOTE OF CAUTION TO THE READER

This book provides information about healing and helping yourself when parenting with a high-conflict co-parent either before, during or after a separation or divorce. The information provided is intended to help you be more educated and aware of how to manage your life more successfully.

Knowledge is power. However, this high-conflict personality information can also be misused, which may inadvertently make your life more difficult. Therefore, we caution you not to publicly label high-conflict people in your life, not to tell people you think they have high-conflict personalities, nor to use this information as a weapon in personal relationships. Before you go further, we ask that you make a commitment to use this information with caution, compassion, and respect.

These explanations and information address general high-conflict behavior and may not apply to your specific situation. You are advised to seek the advice of a professional like a therapist, attorney, or law enforcement officer when warranted.

The authors and publisher are not responsible for any decisions or actions you take as a result of reading this book.

DEDICATIONS

TO THOSE WHO CHALLENGED ME AND THOSE WHO SUPPORTED ME THROUGH THOSE CHALLENGES, THANK YOU.

—ANDREA

DEDICATED TO THE KIDS WHO WILL BENEFIT FROM HEALTHIER PARENTS.

—MEGAN

FOREWORD

by **Bill Eddy, LCSW, Esq.**

When I started reading The High-Conflict Co-Parenting Survival Guide, I was reminded of a study of parenting skills that was done several years ago on what makes a good parent.* After studying hundreds of practices and thousands of parents, two psychologists came up with the top three most important parenting skills:

- Love and affection for your child.
- Ability to manage your own stress.
- Demonstrating healthy relationship skills with your co-parent and other adults.

These results blew everyone away, because they weren't about managing children's behavior, which turned out to be much less important than these top three. Yet these make sense, because children learn more from your example than what you tell them to do. In other words, you can be strict, permissive or make a lot of mistakes, and still be a good parent by demonstrating these three skills. And aiming for these skills is especially important when parents have been in a lot of conflict, such as after a separation or divorce.

That's where this handy guide comes in. It focuses on what you can do to manage your own stress and do your part in demonstrating health relationship skills with your co-parent—even with a high-conflict co-parent. Week after week, Andrea and Megan give useful information combined with soothing and upbeat messages of encouragement.

Their weekly tips will help you stay calm (and regain your calm), so that you are emotionally available for your child and also showing your child how to cope—by your own success at managing your stress. Their weekly tips will also help you stay (or regain) the positive side while reasonably communicating, making decisions and resolving conflicts with other adults in your life.

Just showing your child how well you are surviving this co-parenting business will put them on a good path for life. As the subtitle says, you can Reclaim Your Life One Week at a Time.

----

* Robert Epstein, "What Makes a Good Parent?"
Scientific American Mind, November/December 2010.

Bill Eddy is the developer of the *New Ways for Families®* method and the author of several books, including *Don't Alienate the Kids: Raising Resilient Children While Avoiding High-Conflict Divorce.*

HOW TO USE THIS GUIDE

This survival guide is designed to help you replace fear and chaos with calm and confidence—one week at a time.

This is meant to be a guide to help you deal with and process the intense emotions that come with high-conflict co-parenting.

It's not intended to answer every possible scenario that may come up with your co-parent; rather, it is meant to help you take care of you.

PART 1

Provides information about people who may have high-conflct personalities, and it also contains short-cut tips for improving communication with your co-parent.

PART 2

Is meant for your healing, which begins with

HAVE. FEEL. MOVE

This is the foundation for the entire book. This is a must-read.

WELLNESS ASSESSMENT

Take this self-care assessment to see your strengths and deficits.

CONTINUE TO THE NEXT WEEK'S LESSON

Each week builds on the previous week's lesson, moving you from your core fears and concerns to a place of freedom and control.

WEEKLY LESSONS

Start on Week 1, which you can start any time. After reading the week's lesson, work on:

- Feelings to Move
- Questions
- Challenge
- Take Care Checklist

Work throughout the week on your goals.

MONTHLY CHECK-INS

Check your progress each month and **set new goals** for the coming month

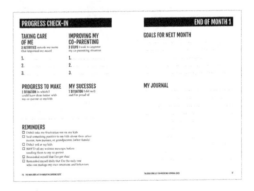

AFTER 52 WEEKS, YOU'RE DONE!

The information is inside the pages of this book. **Now it's up to you!**

YOU CAN START ANY WEEK, ANY TIME, AND WORK THROUGH IT AT YOUR OWN PACE.

INTRODUCTION

Co-parenting with someone who may have a high-conflict personality (HCP) is one of the most challenging issues a divorced or separated parent will face in life.

The terms most often used to describe interactions with HCP co-parents are "dread", "exhausted" and "chaos". People often say they dread communicating with their co-parent because they are exhausted from the chaos.

Anyone would be exhausted if they had to put up with these common HCP co-parenting behaviors:

- screaming
- false allegations of abuse
- child alienation
- endless texts, emails, calls
- public humiliation
- distortion campaigns
- stalking
- recurring court filings
  (we call them frequent filers)
- nagging
- undermining
- lying
- domestic abuse
- blame

A sustained barrage that doesn't allow for a relaxing life. Worse, many children truly suffer emotionally, mentally, and physically, and some have difficulty forming healthy adult relationships as a result.

This book is a wake-up call that you need to start taking care of yourself. You will see how well or sick you are at the beginning and at the end on your weekly journey to becoming a healthier human and parent.

Legal strategies should be left to attorneys and the courts. Taking care of you is up to you, so commit yourself to sticking with the book for 52 weeks. Set a weekly recurring reminder on your calendar and make it part of your routine. You won't regret it!

-The Authors

MEGAN HUNTER, MBA

I am the co-founder and CEO of the High Conflict Institute and founder and publisher of publishing company, Unhooked Media. Both companies focus on helping people in complicated relationships, which ranges from training the professionals who help people through divorce to publishing books for experts who handle divorce and co-parenting cases. Prior to developing the concept of having an institute that focuses solely on high-conflict personalities, I was a child support enforcement caseworker in Nebraska and the Child Support Specialist and Family Law Specialist at the Arizona Supreme Court, Administrative Office of the Courts. Along this path I became keenly aware of what I believe to be a public health crisis—high-conflict divorce—and the toll it takes on children, parents, the system, and society.

My work focuses solely on helping people understand how those on the higher end of the high-conflict spectrum operate and how to handle relationships in any form with them. With this book, my focus broadens to the wellness of the parent who must deal long-term with a high-conflict co-parent.

In my personal life, I have been divorced and have co-parented very successfully with my co-parent. Our divorce and co-parenting could have been ugly, but we learned how to communicate over the years. Although no relationship is perfect, I think we did pretty good and have been able to compliment each other on our co-parenting success now that our kids are grown.

ANDREA LAROCHELLE

YOU KNOW THAT FEELING YOU GET WHEN...

you thought you were plugging away at life, boundaries in place and a tiny window of calm takes over your life? It's the best feeling in the whole world and you plan to do everything you can to keep that feeling? **Then WHAM!**

Out of nowhere, your co-parent does/says something and your calm becomes anger, fear, anxiety, a puddle of tears and/or utter exhaustion? And just like that, you can't remember what the calm felt like? I HATE WHEN THAT HAPPENS.

In my head, that calm place is where I thought happiness was. Freedom. The life I wasn't living but so desperately wanted to be living. Because it was my co-parent that triggered me out of that calm place, I directed all my negative feelings about being taken out of my calm place in their direction.

I blamed THEM. For how I was feeling, and just like that, I was behaving exactly like how I was complaining they were behaving. That's not me, not my authentic self, not my calm self. It would feel like I was living in someone else's body, with someone else's thoughts and behaviors. It kind of felt like I was a raging lunatic who had no control over my words or actions. I would find myself snapping at my kids, then feeling enormous guilt and shame about the freak out I didn't need to have. My 7-year-old once said to me, "Just because someone hurt your feelings, doesn't mean you should hurt mine." OUCH.

How did my 7-year-old become more emotionally intelligent/competent than me? But it was the slap in the face I needed to take control of who I was, to explore my role in my co-parenting conflict.

I always say to clients who just want to know if they are the high-conflict parent—because if they are, they promise to do whatever I say to change.

"If you are asking me if you are the high-conflict parent, chances are good you aren't because you had the insight to question yourself and your actions. BUT, you could be contributing to the ongoing conflict by the way you respond to your co-parent's insults, accusations, manipulations and lies."

Many clients stop listening at "...chances are good you're not..." and completely ignore the "... you could be contributing to the conflict..." OR they will breathe a sigh of relief and then ask me how to change from reacting to responding to the onslaught of horrific'ness sent their way on an hourly/daily/weekly basis. I would give them the tools they needed to communicate with someone who lacks insight into their own behavior and appears to have very little emotional intelligence.

Clients would leave my office feeling empowered to do differently. They would have the self-confidence to create and implement boundaries. They felt ready to manage their own emotions so that their co-parent couldn't control them anymore.

Inevitably, I would get an email a week or a month later from that same take-charge-of-my-life client telling me my strategies didn't work, that their co-parent continues to harass, control and manipulate not only them but the kids as well. The strategies work so I had to dig a little further to find out what went sideways. I would have my client forward me a few email chains so I could review them to see where things derailed and voilà—before getting through the first email—I would know exactly why my client was struggling. They had been triggered and had re-engaged.

WHAT DOES RE-ENGAGED LOOK LIKE?

The Cycle of Hope: Getting their hopes up when their co-parent was nice for a few days that maybe they could have a white picket fence divorce then getting taken out at the knees when the old awful behavior returns. Hope, disappointment, hope, disappointment. It's a vicious, soul crushing cycle.

- Attack/Defend Behavior
- Long winded, pleading emails
- Trying to give the co-parent insight
- Giving opinions about the kids in emails
- Texting hurricanes
- Losing sleep
- Lack of productivity at home/work
- Strategizing on how to fix the situation:
- And the list goes on...

I knew the communication strategies worked, when implemented, and I knew how to help people feel their self-worth and move to a place of "I can do this!"

But it wasn't sustainable.

People were going back to their old communication patterns as soon as they were triggered, which meant that my disengaging tools weren't working for them, there was something more that my clients needed to help them out of their high-conflict hell and into their life.

WHICH BRINGS ME TO THIS *HIGH-CONFLICT CO-PARENTING SURVIVAL GUIDE.*

I knew from my own experience with a high-conflict person that there are many layers of healing that need to take place to fully disengage and live without hate. Live without hate??? Say whaaaaaat? It's coming... each time I thought I had successfully conquered disengagement, the universe would not so gently tap me on the shoulder (or give me an elbow to the head) to remind me not to be so arrogant with my calm and disengaged state.

It's been 6 years since I started the disengagement process from the high-conflict person in my life. Six years of untangling the web of toxic emotional patterns I created for survival while that person was still living in my home. Six years of learning, feeling, falling apart, waking up and trying to piece myself back together. It has been its own little slice of hell. Dipped in chocolate. Dipped in chocolate you ask? Yes. Because for every ounce of awfulness that the HCP in my life brought to my world, the insight and awareness that grew from each storm cannot be matched.

I used to dream of going back to the person I was before I had the HCP in life; the carefree, light and easy-going personality that was engaging and fun. Fun. During the ugly years, fun didn't exist in my life. I would romanticize who I was 'then' and criticize who I was 'now' and blame my HCP. I managed to do all that without even realizing I was doing it! Our minds are fascinating places!

It took some time and some healing and some self exploration, but I now understand that I didn't want to go back in time and be the person I was – I just wanted to 'feel' the way I used to feel. Once I learned that it was a feeling I was after, I learned I could consciously create those feelings without having to go back in time.

But the storm before the insight is dark, cold, lonely, terrifying and more crazy making than anyone who has never experienced an HCP could ever imagine. That's part of what makes the HCP so powerful in their manipulations against us. No one else understands.

For years clients have been asking that I write about the 'other side', what it's like to move through the misery of co-parenting with an HCP. "How did you do it?" they would ask. I've resisted because I haven't felt ready. I didn't think I had the answers or the plan or the insight or the... then I realized that that was the old me, the me who 'wasn't good enough' in my HCP's eyes. The old me who thought she couldn't do anything right, who created this bizarre world that everything had to be perfect, which is ironic because nothing in the eyes of an HCP is perfect... which just feeds the 'never good enough' narrative.

It's been 6 years. Six years of research, seminars, reading, conferences, writing and practicing the evolvement of disengaging. Because that is what disengagement is all about – evolvement. As you evolve, you will further disengage. As you disengage, you will further evolve. (ying/yang).

I'm ready now, I'm ready to share with you how I put my pieces back together to make an even stronger, more awesome me. An even lighter, more engaged 'fun' me.

How you, too, can stop being a shell of yourself and become an even stronger, more awesome you. Regardless of the sh*t storm going around you.

How to be someone you love. Someone your kids admire. Someone who has been missing for far too long It's going to take some effort on your part. There is no magic pill. No wand I can wave. Trust me, I tried. You name it, I tried it.

I had health issues (turns out all stress related, who knew stress could give you step throat? FOR 6 MONTHS STRAIGHT!!!), weight issues, friendship issues, familial issues, burn out, depression, anxiety, overwhelm, compassion fatigue, decision making fatigue and all-encompassing feelings of "I can't do this anymore" and "There has got to be something I can do to fix this."

I tried counselling, medical doctors, naturopaths, acupuncture, napping, writing, shopping, eating, quitting my job (repeatedly) – anything and everything to try and find something outside of myself to help me heal. Then one day one of the many naturopaths I had seen said, "Andrea, there is nothing medically wrong causing your symptoms.

I think you need to look inwards." SHOOT.

Enter metaphorical brick to the head telling me to WAKE UP. While I liked to think of myself as emotionally intelligent, intuitively savvy and empathically strong – self-help was a hobby of mine for a very long time – the truth was, I was only skimming the surface. Once I understood the characteristics of an HCP and that I wasn't crazy, I peeled off a layer of hurt and plowed forward with my new skills for communicating.

But it turns out there is more than one layer of hurt. Even though I continued to be triggered, EVEN THOUGH I KNEW THE SKILLS, it forced me to unravel further. To figure out how to really evolve into disengagement and not just disengage on the surface.

That mysterious feeling of calm that I thought was happiness? I was wrong. Happiness is not a destination feeling. Happiness is understanding your triggers and your response patterns, continuously evolving into disengagement and living authentically regardless of what feeling your body may be having at any given time. Happiness is trusting that the horrible feelings will pass. No feeling is permanent, unless you attach a story to the feeling, stories are harder to move than feelings.

Freedom is the feeling of unconditional love. For yourself. It's not an easy journey, and it's certainly not a road that's frequently travelled (Shout Out to Robert Frost's poem "The Road Less Travelled").

IF YOU KNOW IN YOUR GUT THAT THERE HAS GOT TO BE MORE TO LIFE THAN THE HORRIFIC'NESS THAT YOU ARE CURRENTLY LIVING WITH?

Then you're in the right place. **Reading the right book.**

HAVE. FEEL. MOVE

It's next to impossible to use flexible thinking to moderate your behavior if you haven't learned to manage your emotions.

Common negative emotions—anger, fear, anxiety, stress, worry, frustration, resentment, sorrow, sadness, desperation and hate—when not managed, can create havoc in your life. A high-conflict divorce is the perfect catalyst to create all of those negative emotions, often times all at once.

A stressed-out parent isn't easily able to moderate their behavior when a child accidentally drops a glass of milk on the floor. A parent full of hate won't be able to use flexible thinking to understand the benefits that both parents can offer in their child's life. Living in fear that someone may criticize or use their actions against them will reduce a parent's ability to allow their children to grow and flourish. An anxious parent breeds an anxious home and an anxious child. Anxiety takes away the ability to be truly happy and content.

Negative emotions take a toll on the body, mind and spirit. Physical health starts to deteriorate—sore knees, stiff neck, repeated throat infections, and weakened immune system. Your brain feels foggy, you become forgetful, focusing on anything for more than a few minutes is challenging. It becomes more and more difficult to find joy in day-to-day living, you're laughing less and snapping more, you start to avoid social gatherings.

These are just the short-term implications, but what about the long-term effects of stress on your health? Evidence clearly links trauma and stress to many mid-life and later-life physical problems such as autoimmune disorders, heart disease, and others.

Very few people know how to manage their emotions effectively, especially their negative ones.

WE TRY A VARIETY OF EMOTION MANAGERS:

- Go for a run
- Take a brisk walk
- Have a glass of wine
- Eat a piece of chocolate
- Watch a funny movie
- Hit a pillow or scream into it
- Just let it go

If any of those easy fixes worked, why are we still wandering around unable to manage our emotions effectively? When you've been triggered into anger, just letting it go doesn't work. When you're so anxious you can't sit still, watching a funny movie isn't going to calm you. When you're trying to control everything around you because you can't control the one thing you desperately want to control, eating a piece of chocolate isn't going to magically make you feel better. When you are so lost, exhausted and bewildered at your current situation that you feel paralyzed, a glass of wine isn't going to help energize you so you can change strategies.

SO WHAT DOES WORK? WHAT CAN YOU DO TO HELP YOU MANAGE YOUR EMOTIONS?

No, you can't move to Mars and disappear; you can't relocate to New York and start over; and you can't change who had a child with. While appealing, this wishful thinking isn't reality. You want to know how to manage your emotions so that your emotions don't manage you.

Emotions are powerful. They come, they go. Sometimes they overstay their welcome. At some point in life we learned to let our emotions become our identity. As a child you may have heard a parent or teacher state that you were an anxious, angry or depressed child, although you didn't feel anxious, angry or depressed. Somehow you became an anxious, angry, depressed child.

Or as an adult you may have adopted some negative emotions because of certain life experiences or traumatic events you've been through. "He's been angry since started he lost his job." "She's been anxious since they separated." "She's been walking around with her head in the clouds since her sister passed away."

Everyone responds differently to emotions, both negative and positive. For example, anger can be expressed through tears, screaming, laughing, silence, suppression, or scheming. There is no right way to be angry; it's a feeling that everyone has now and then. Some of us more often than others. Sorrow can be expressed through the very same expressions as anger: tears, screaming, laughing, silence, suppression, or scheming. There is nothing wrong with having those feelings. It's normal to HAVE them.

HAVE is the key.
HAVE the feeling.
FEEL the feeling.
MOVE the feeling.
HAVE. FEEL. MOVE.
Most people tend to HAVE a feeling.
Fewer people FEEL the feeling.
Almost no one MOVES the feeling.

WE'VE ALL BEEN THERE

That moment when you snap from a calm, sane human being to an irrational, screaming nut-head. That conversation that was going smoothly until suddenly it wasn't. You burst into tears out of frustration or feel the anger rising within and you can't regain composure. Those circles you keep walking in, unable to figure out why your words only seem to make the situation worse. That paralyzing anxiety that stops you from creating or implementing any real boundaries. That silly goofiness that takes over when you think you simply can't continue with the craziness that has become your life.

We've all had that eternally optimistic friend or family member who only sees life through rose-colored glasses:

- "... life throws us curve balls to challenge us"
- "... what doesn't kill you makes you stronger"
- "... life is giving us the tools we need to move forward"

Yadda yadda yadda—maybe you'd buy into the rose-colored glasses if you could see some kind of light at the end of the tunnel, but there is no light in sight. Instead, you see a long dark space that feels like it's slowly sucking the life out of you.

You can't change who you had kids with. You can't change the condescending and manipulative tone they use towards you. You can't change the often-cruel steps taken to hurt you regardless of who else it hurts in the processes. So what can you do?

You can take responsibility for your own feelings using the Have, Feel, Move method.

HAVE

Professionals talk about feelings being a choice. They suggest that you are choosing to be angry and that you can choose to be less angry. Obviously, they've never been really and truly angry. The kind of angry that makes you think your head might start spinning like the girl from the Exorcist movie. I like to call real anger 'Exorcist Anger'. Exorcist Anger makes you feel like your blood is boiling; it stops all rational thought; makes you feel like you will either pass out or throw things.

Exorcist Anger is not a choice—it's a physical reaction to real and/or imagined circumstances. Exorcist Anger is physical.

You can't stop the fact that your body has reacted to something or someone. Your body decides whether or not it will have Exorcist Anger. This is where we often get stuck. The body has a reaction to something or someone and then they have Exorcist Anger. The same example can be used for any emotion: your body decides to have anxiety, have worry, have giddiness, and have resentment. Emotions are not a choice they are a reaction.

FEEL

THIS IS WHERE FEELING BECOMES A CHOICE.

Where you choose to be angry, sad, resentful or anxious. Since the time when we were young, we have been conditioned not to feel. When you fell and scraped your knee, you were told to get up and brush it off. When you cried because you didn't get picked for the basketball team, you were told to suck it up and stop crying. When someone told you to stop being sad after little Johnny or Kylie hurt your feelings. When you were told that life isn't fair so stop being angry when your sister got the bigger piece of birthday cake... on your birthday. We are conditioned from a young age not to feel our feelings.

Somewhere in history feelings became something to fear, to avoid, or to squash. But something has to happen to that physical response you had to something or someone. If you don't feel your feelings, you'll either get stuck in having them or find feeling masks. Some people eat their feelings. Others smoke their feelings.

Some do drugs, create sex addictions, become hoarders or perfectionists. It's that simple. If you get stuck in having feelings and don't learn to feel your feelings, they will start to feel you.

So how, after years or decades of not feeling feelings, do you learn to actually feel? The answer is easy, but it takes a lot of practice, and planning, because when you're triggered into having a feeling, your rational thought processes go out the window.

You have to have a plan. You have to know what you are going to do the next time you are triggered into anger, worry, resentment, or sadness. If you don't have a plan, you'll get stuck in HAVE instead of moving from HAVE to FEEL.

You need to start recognizing how, when and why you get triggered into having a feeling. Here's how you can start!

STEPS TO MOVE FROM HAVE TO FEEL

1. Start recognizing HOW, WHEN and WHY you get triggered into HAVING a feeling.

2. What happens to you physically when you get angry? Do you have an anxiety attack? Fall into sadness? Shut down? It is vitally important to become aware of your physical reactions to the feelings you are having. Once you know your physical reactions to HAVING a feeling, you can learn to FEEL the feeling.

3. When you are triggered into a feeling, get down and dirty with the physical reaction your body is having. Triggered into Exorcist Anger? Go ahead and FEEL every ounce of blood pumping through your veins, and get lost in that dizzy feeling you get because all the blood has left your brain; or excuse yourself and go somewhere safe and private to throw things, punch a heavy weight bag, or pound a table with your fist.

4. Give yourself 5 minutes to feel every last ounce of anger, sadness, worry or resentment your body has been triggered into having. Seriously, set a timer. FEELING your emotions for 5 minutes is hard. Our head wants to take over and start thinking, planning, strategizing. But if you're thinking, you're not feeling. If you're not feeling, you're getting stuck in having. You have been programmed into getting stuck in HAVING, so getting into feeling will be a challenge. Do it anyway.

MOVE

YOU WANT ME TO WHAT?

Yes, now you must MOVE your feelings.
HAVE them.
FEEL them.
MOVE them.

If you choose not to MOVE your feelings, you will continue to be triggered by the same things that have triggered you in the past. If you are continually being triggered by the same people or events that triggered you in the past, you are not moving forward. If you're not moving forward, you are stuck.

When you get stuck, you probably feel like you are a fish in a mud puddle.

We need to move to stay alive, but it feels like so much work to get anywhere. Being stuck feels hopeless, depressed, lost and tired.

Jump out of the mud puddle. Get unstuck. MOVE your feelings.

Does it sound difficult to MOVE your feelings? It's not when you do it using the Two-Minute Tango! It's actually quite easy and effective. If it sounds too easy, try it and stick with it because it works! Schedule the Two-Minute Tango into your day like you would any meeting. Two minutes, twice a day.

STEPS TO MOVE FROM HAVE TO FEEL

TWO-MINUTE TANGO PREP:

1. Grab a timer or set the timer on your phone
2. Set the timer to go off every 24 seconds
3. Start the Two-Minute Tango

TWO-MINUTE TANGO:

- Yawn repeatedly for 24 seconds
- Scream as loud and as hard as you can for 24 seconds
- Laugh hysterically from your gut for 24 seconds
- Cry like you just lost your best friend for 24 seconds
- Shake your body like it's a human vibrator for 24 seconds

You will feel better, lighter, and clearer afterwards. Don't create resistance to doing it in an attempt to sabotage yourself from feeling better. You are comfortable in your safe space of anger, anxiety, and sadness. Safe isn't going to help you help you manage your emotions or moderate your behavior so that you can use flexible thinking to move forward.

Safe is going to keep you stuck in having conflict.
Safe is going to keep you stuck in having anger.
Safe is going to keep you stuck having anxiety.
What have you got to lose?
4 minutes a day?
Have. Feel. Move.

HIGH-CONFLICT STRATEGIES

Spending two or three decades of your life dealing with a high-conflict co-parent impacts your daily life, eats away at your sanity, your peace of mind, your friendships and other relationships, and the joy of a conflict-free life with your kids.

Worse, your kids may be turned against you, domestic violence or abuse happens, or you may be slandered by a distortion campaign at your workplace, in your community, or within your own family.

The impact on you as the parent is devastating, but the impact on the kids can be worse as it affects them long beyond childhood. Research clearly demonstrates that exposing kids to high-conflict influence negatively impacts their adult relationships, mental health, and even their physical health. An entire industry has sprung up around high-conflict divorce and co-parenting in an attempt to protect children.

You may be a parent who has taken your kids to the doctor after the school calls about your child's ongoing stomach pain, disruptive behavior, poor grades, or depression. They start medicating or therapizing: ADHD medication, stomach pills, or direction to visit a therapist or psychiatrist. The court appoints numerous professionals to look after the child's best interest, but it just never seems to end.

The accusations begin rolling in and your life is spent protecting yourself, trying to guess what your next move should be. The stress is relentless and the fear debilitating. You may turn to the court or your lawyer for help, but they can only do so much.

You are in survival mode, putting one foot in front of the other while trying to put food on the table and trying to achieve some normalcy. You may have given up or given in, electing to forego a relationship with your kids to protect them from conflict. Or you may have engaged in the battle but keep running into roadblocks.

Don't beat yourself up if you are in survival mode and don't know exactly how to proceed. This book is for you to turn things around and to begin managing the co-parenting relationship instead of letting it manage and overwhelm you.

You must remain engaged in taking care of and protecting your kids while taking care of yourself, but life is too short to let a past relationship destroy your present or future.

What follows is a list of resources for parents involved in high-conflct divorce, separation or custody disputes. These are just a few resources available. We do not recommend one over another. Take your time to research each resource to determine if it applies to your situation and if it will help your family as it transitions over the years.

TALKING AND WRITING

Communication will make or break the relationship between co-parents. There's a right way and a wrong way to talk and to write. Before diving into the 52-week survival guide, read this brief communication guide, practice it, and come back to it weekly when you get frustrated by the endless texts, calls, emails, and in-person discussions.

TALKING

Your co-parent's brain needs to feel safe. It doesn't want to feel threatened, even though it frequently does. When it feels threatened it reacts aggressively with insults, yelling, accusations, and put-downs. Then you react and the conversation spirals once again.

How to Talk to Your Co-Parent (in person or over the phone)

Calm Voice
- keep your voice calm at all times
- keep your voice quiet – do not raise your voice
- keep contempt out of your voice
- keep a condescending tone out of your voice
- don't sigh
- use words and phrases that show empathy, attention, and respect (this is called an EAR Statement☐, which was developed by Bill Eddy, LCSW, Esq.)

Nonchalant Face
- keep your facial expressions pleasant
- don't roll your eyes
- don't smack your forehead in exasperation
- smile if you can

Non-threatening Body Language
- keep your arms uncrossed
- keep your hands off your hips
- avoid giving them the finger
- threatening body posture

You are the one in charge of communication. Use your voice, face, and body language to keep things calm when you must communicate.

Instead of texting, use a tech-based communication tool like OurFamilyWizard.com or ProperComm.com if you can get your co-parent to agree to it or the court to order it.

What to avoid
- arguing
- endlessly defending yourself
- endlessly explaining your actions
- accusing
- blaming
- putting your co-parent on blast on social media (in other words, don't complain or share your frustrations on social media)

It's tempting to do any of these things because you are frustrated and want to be heard. You're wasting your time and energy. Put that time and energy into taking care of yourself and your children.

HOW TO WRITE LETTERS, TEXTS, AND EMAILS TO YOUR CO-PARENT

Bill Eddy, LCSW, Esq. developed a method called BIFF Response® for responding to hostile written communications like texts, emails, and letters, especially with people who have high-conflict personalities. It works. Try it, practice it, and use it in every written communication with your co-parent.

Step 1
Decide whether you need to respond or not.

Step 2
If you need to respond, slow it down and respond instead of react. Use this format:

Brief: keep it brief. You don't need to respond to every accusation or allegation. Most allegations and accusations are verbal vomit in written form, and once they've been expelled, they're forgotten. Meanwhile, you ruminate and let it get under your skin. Don't. Instead, only respond to anything that requires a response in order to get something done, like picking a meeting spot.
Bill recommends one paragraph of 2-5 sentences maximum. If it's more, cut it down.

Informative: when you've narrowed down what you absolutely need to respond to, keep your response factual and informative. Remove judgment, blame, accusations and hostility from your response. Just stick to boring, basic facts.

Friendly: keep it the tone friendly. Not over-the-top friendly, but just keep a friendly, non-threatening tone with politeness. Use thank you, please, and use EAR (empathy, attention, respect) when you can.

Firm: keeping it firm does not mean using threats or big demands. The goal of keeping it firm is to end the conversation and stop further emails or texts on the topic. Instead, you may be setting a boundary or closing the conversation by keeping it firm. You can say that this is all you are going to say on the subject.
Then, if they write back, you don't have to respond. If you need to continue the communication, give 2 options for them to choose from and set a reply by date.

Step 3
Check it to ensure you haven't used one or more of the **Three A's:** advice, admonishments, apologies.

Advice just brings up your co-parent's defenses.

Admonishments do the same.

Apologies make them feel like they're completely right and you are completely wrong. Just avoid them.

Step 4
Wait to send it until you've had time to reconsider it after a good night's sleep. By the time you look at it again, your emotions may be much lower and you'll see it more clearly. Emotions are influencers on communications. You want to respond with logic instead of emotion.

Responding with a **BIFF Response®** can seem counter-intuitive, but it's the magic wand of written communications with a high-conflict co-parent. It will make your life easier and way less stressful. Try it. You can do it, but it will take some practice. Remind yourself to BIFF all of your written communications when you need to respond to in writing or if you have an important letter to write to your co-parent.

HERE'S AN EXAMPLE

from *BIFF Quick Responses to High-Conflict People, Their Personal Attacks, Hostile Email, and Social Media Meltdowns* (2014) (copied with permission from Bill Eddy, LCSW, Esq. and High Conflict Institute Press).

It's six months since Erik and Connie's divorce was finished. But they still have routine parenting issues that come up from time to time. Some of them become fights.

Consider the following issue and then write a BIFF response for Erik to send to Connie after the email exchange below:

> **Erik:** I'd like to have Wally on Tuesday evening, June 14th, to attend a father-son baseball game that our group has organized. I know it's usually your night, but I'd like to have this night. I'm willing to switch with another night, in order to be flexible.

> **Connie:** Erik, you have not been helping Wally enough with his homework on his school nights! I will end your weekday overnights if you don't spend at least two hours helping him study on both of your weekday parenting nights. I want you to keep a record of the exact hours that he spends studying while he is at your house. You know I thought this parenting arrangement wouldn't work out, and it hasn't!!! And you know it!!!

Note that she never actually responded to Erik's request. She changed the subject. This is common with HCPs, who cannot let the other person seem to be in charge of any interaction.

Now, check to see if your response is Brief, Informative, Friendly and Firm. Then, check to see if your response has any admonishments, advice and/or apologies in it.

Here's one way of writing it, but remember there is no one right way. Your BIFF needs to fit the unique current situation, which you know more about than anyone else.

> **Hi Connie,**
>
> Thanks for responding to my request right away.
>
> I understand your concern that Wally gets his homework done and I share that concern. I can have him work on his homework immediately after school is out, so that he has it done before the game on Tuesday. I can discuss the importance of that with him during our time together this weekend.
>
> I understand that changing days between parents is a routine matter and I am open to changing days with you when there are special mother-son events.
>
> I believe it will make us both look good. With this new information in mind about my commitment to getting the homework done first, I will plan on picking him up from school on Tuesday, unless you tell me otherwise right away. Thanks for considering the benefits to Wally of us being flexible.
>
> Erik

If you think it's BIFF'd enough, BIFF it again. Have a trusted friend BIFF it even more.

ONLINE COURSES

New Ways for Families® Online
www.newways4families.com/pwc

12-HOUR COURSE FOR PARENTS

- An online course available to anyone, anywhere, anytime
- Developed by Bill Eddy, LCSW, Esq., who developed the high-conflct personality theory and is the co-founder and Training Director of the High Conflict Institute
- Teaches much-needed relationship and self-calming skills that rely on evidence-based methods that are proven to help people learn to manage their own emotions, have moderate behaviors, and flexible thinking
- 12 sessions

GOALS:

- To help parents teach their children skills for resilience during this time of huge and rapid change in the foundation of their family life. These skills serve children for a lifetime.
- To strengthen both parents' abilities to resolve their co-parenting conflicts and make parenting decisions together, while relying less on the courts and other professionals to make decisions for them.
- assist professionals in assessing each parent's willingness and ability to engage in learning and applying new skills for the benefit of their children.
- To give parents a chance to change their behavior, prior to the court making long-term orders (can be used at any point in the co-parenting time period)
- To encourage mediation or another alternative dispute resolution process to make co-parenting decisions

4-HOUR COURSE FOR PARENTS AND KIDS

- Designed for parents in the beginning, middle or end of their divorce or separation process or any time during ongoing co-parenting.
- Includes activities that parents can do with their child throughout each of the classes, with each class focused on one skill. The course provides lots of tips for easy ways to teach children these concepts. Many of the activities focus on helping the child with a simple activity, such as putting pictures from magazines into a scrapbook or on a paper bag with examples of children and adults using these skills. The activities will help the parent discuss with the child which behaviors are okay (moderate behavior) in a situation and which behaviors are not acceptable (extreme behavior).
- Sample language: the course includes examples of words parents can use to explain concepts to their child, as well as questions parents can ask their child to help get these discussions going.
- The five general age groups: All activities, discussion questions, sample language, and examples are provided for each of the following age groups: 0-3 years 4-6 years 7-11 years 12-17 years 18-25 years

GOALS:

- Teach the child to use the 4 BIG Skills during this time of rapid change
- Make the parent-child relationship stronger and less stressful, opening the door for honest and supportive conversation about the future
- Help the parent guide their child through this time of transition with less stress, less anxiety, and a more stable foundation for moving forward

BOOKS

All books can be found at any bookstore or online, and some are available as e-books and audio books.

Don't Alienate the Kids:
Raising Resilient Children While
Avoiding High Conflict Divorce
Bill Eddy, LCSW, Esq.

Splitting:
Protecting Yourself While Divorcing
Someone with Borderline or Narcissistic
Personality Disorder
Bill Eddy, LCSW, Esq.
with **Randi Kreger**

Overcoming the Co-Parenting Trap:
Essential Parenting Skills When
A Child Resists A Parent
Matt Sullivan, PhD,
John Moran, PhD,
Tyler Sullivan

CoParenting After Divorce
Debra Carter

High Conflict People in Legal Disputes
Bill Eddy, LCSW, Esq.

The Healthy Parenting Series
Benjamin D. Garber, PhD

1. *The Healthy Parent's ABCs:*
   Healthy Parenting Made Clear
   and Easy-to-Read
2. *Taming the Beast Within:*
   Managing Anger in Ourselves and
   in Our Children Through Divorce
3. *Caught in the Middle:*
   A Letter to My Divorced Parents

BIFF
Quick Responses to High-Conflict
People, Their Hostile Email, Personal
Attacks, and Social Media Meltdowns
Bill Eddy, LCSW, Esq.

Divorce Poison:
How To Protect Your Family from
Bad-mouthing and Brainwashing
Richard Warshak, PhD

Parenting a Child Who
Has Intense Emotions
Pat Harvey, LCSW

Parenting a Teen Who
Has Intense Emotions
Pat Harvey, LCSW

ON-SITE PROGRAMS FOR FAMILIES

Overcoming Barriers
www.overcomingbarriers.org

Transitioning Families
www.transitioningfamilies.com

ProperComm
www.propercomm.com

VIDEOS FOR PARENTS & KIDS

Welcome Back, Pluto
www.warshak.com/pluto/trailer.html

Split:
A Film for Kids of Divorce
(and their Parents)
www.splitfilm.org

LET'S GET STARTED...

WELLNESS ASSESSMENT

KNOWING WHERE YOU ARE TODAY WILL HELP YOU KNOW WHAT TO SHOOT FOR IN YOUR SURVIVAL JOURNEY.

USING THIS SCALE, RATE THE FOLLOWING AREAS IN TERMS OF FREQUENCY

5 Frequently

4 Occasionally

3 Rarely

2 Never

1 It never occurred to me

PSYCHOLOGICAL WELLNESS

Write in a journal	
Go to a therapist	
Read books unrelated to work	
Take time to self-reflect	
Intentionally decrease stress in your life	
Track your emotions	
Let someone else be in charge	

SPIRITUAL WELLNESS

Have a spiritual community	
Spend time outdoors	
Be aware of nonmaterial aspects of life	
Pray	
Sing	
Volunteer to teach Sunday School or work with youth	
Read inspirational literature (talks, music, etc.)	

EMOTIONAL WELLNESS

Spend time with people you feel comfortable around	
Stay in touch with important people in your life	
Give yourself affirmations, praise yourself, love yourself	
Get out of the house	
Re-read favorite books, re-view favorite movies	
Allow yourself to cry	
Find things that make you laugh	

THIS WELLNESS ASSESSMENT WILL GIVE YOU A CLEAR PICTURE OF HOW WELL YOU ARE TAKING CARE OF YOURSELF AND AREAS WHERE YOU NEED TO IMPROVE. AFTER TAKING THIS BRIEF ASSESSMENT, YOU WILL BE READY TO DIVE INTO WEEK 1.

PHYSICAL WELLNESS

- Eat nutritious foods and have a consistent eating schedule
- Exercise (hike, dance, swim, walk, run, play sports, yoga)
- Get regular preventive medical care and get medical care when needed
- Get consistent sleep
- Take time off when needed (vacations, weekend trips)
- Get massages, pedicures, manicures
- Take a day per week away from technology

INSIGHT WELLNESS

- Allow others to know different sides or aspects of you
- Notice your inner experiences like processing and listening to your attitudes, beliefs, feelings, thoughts
- Do something new like going camping, to a museum, fishing, sporting events, auction, theater, etc.
- Allow others to help you
- Be curious
- Say "no" on occasion when asked to help

WORK WELLNESS

- Take breaks during the workday
- Take time to chat with co-workers
- Recognize when you are working too many hours
- Recognize when you are taking on too much
- Set limits with co-workers, customers, clients
- Arrange your work space so it's comfortable/comforting

"HOW DID THIS HAPPEN TO ME?"

How did I get into this mess?
Co-parenting with someone who appears to be on a singular mission to destroy me, seemingly unaware of what they are doing to our kids in the process?

HOW DID I MISS THE SIGNS? WERE THERE SIGNS?

Do you spend hours, days, even years dissecting your past to try and pinpoint exactly when and things went sideways? Trying to figure out the exact moment you knew things weren't perfect but you glazed over those feelings because you believed in your partner? You knew that if you loved them enough they would be able to see their own potential? That in your heart of hearts you knew that deep down they were a good person, but they just needed help learning how amazing they are?

If you find yourself asking how this happened to you, then you are still trying to control the future with events from the past. You are unconsciously (or consciously) trying to rewrite your history in an attempt to save yourself (and your kids) from the present circumstances.

Read that line again: "... then you are still trying to control the future with events from the past."

If you're stuck trying to change the past to control your future, you're stuck in a puddle of quick-hardening cement. And if you're in quick-hardening cement? You will never feel the freedom, calm, and peace you are craving. You will never get past the misery you are currently experiencing.

It may sound cliché, but we can say with 100% certainty that you can't change your past. And believe us, we've tried—relentlessly, and we've helped many who've been caught in the same mindset.

When we keep doing the same thing over and over, without positive results, it's called a response pattern.

Response patterns are thoughts, feelings and/or actions we've created to keep us safe, to keep us in our comfort zone, to protect us from the mystical question "What if?" Which makes ZERO sense because often times response patterns are shame, guilt, anger and fear. Or over-eating, drinking wine every night, trying to control the past or the future. Or repeatedly asking yourself, "How did this happen to me?" hoping to secure a different history so that your present and future wouldn't involve your co-parent.

THAT'S CALLED WISHFUL THINKING.

Response patterns are created subconsciously to help us manage and cope with trauma in our lives. We don't choose our response patterns consciously. In fact, most of us aren't even aware of them.

Make no mistake, high-conflict co-parenting is traumatic. Physically, emotionally, mentally, spiritually, and energetically.

> **TRAUMA:** a nightmare of thoughts, images and emotions based on past wounds or hurts that create unconscious and irrational stress in the body that suspends awareness of our infinite nature.
> **—MASTIN KIPP**

In an attempt to manage the trauma we are repeatedly faced with, we create response patterns to keep us safe. They don't actually keep us safe--it's a façade, but they definitely help keep us stuck in a cycle of one step forward, one step back, which is essentially being stuck in cement. Being stuck feels AWFUL!

You've felt awful long enough. You've given your power to outside forces that don't deserve it. You've sacrificed your well-being. You've desperately tried to fix a situation that can't be fixed. You've been trapped in your response patterns with no obvious exit.

Now it's time to escape and reclaim your power, your confidence, and your love of life. It's time to not only survive your high-conflict co-parenting relationship, it's time to thrive through it. And that, dear parent, is the unicorn of feelings—freedom. So let's start moving the feelings! (check page 14 for a reminder on how to move feelings)

FEELINGS TO MOVE

- ☐ Fear
- ☐ Anger
- ☐ Worry
- ☐ Surrender
- ☐ Over-excitement.

QUESTIONS

1. What response patterns are you currently aware of?
2. How have they kept you safe?
3. What have they kept you safe from?

CHALLENGE

Pay attention to the feelings that arise and the patterns you have created when you're triggered.

TAKE CARE CHECKLIST

- ☐ How much sleep are you getting?
- ☐ How often do you get into nature?
- ☐ Have you taken a bath, Jacuzzi or sauna?
- ☐ Have you completed the Trigger Challenge?
- ☐ Are you spending time with friends?
- ☐ When was the last time you read a book for pleasure?
- ☐ Have you taken a walk recently?
- ☐ How often do you move your body?
- ☐ Are you eating well?
- ☐ Do you mediate? Yoga?

YOU DON'T NEED FIXING

You're told you are worthless, fat, a liar, manipulative, that your mother raised you horribly, that you have no friends. That you are overwhelmed making you useless as a parent...

You're told if you would just fix your personality, your body shape, your past, who your family is, how you talk, walk, and think, your unique traits that make you unique, your co-parent (or spouse if you were or are married to them) wouldn't be forced to be as mean or erratic as they are.

Or they are completely dependent on you as if their life depended on your ability to be there every second of every day for them. It's all about them, all the time.

You're told it's your fault they treat you the way they treat you. You're blamed for everything. You're told that events happened that you know didn't happen, or vice versa.

You've been so mentally and emotionally beaten down or worn down that a part of you starts to believe their words. So you begin the process to start trying to fix yourself. Trying to make you the person they want you to be. You read self-help books, go on every diet known to man, go to a life coach, parenting coach or therapist to figure out what you're doing wrong, or you may even distance yourself from your family. You're walking on eggshells.

But each time you fix something about yourself, they come up with something else about you that needs fixing. You can't keep up. You start to believe that you're so broken and need so much fixing that you aren't worthy of being loved, of having a great job, of being the kind of person you know you want to be. Or even if you are secure in those areas, you are simply exhausted from trying to figure them out, from defending yourself or explaining your actions or lack of action.

The list of what you need to fix becomes so long that your co-parent starts to point out that you're slacking on fixing. You sink further into your misery.

Occasionally you give your head a shake, talk to a few friends or counselors who point out the error in logic behind your co-parent's criticisms—but that clarity is short-lived because the next ALL CAPS email from your co-parent is filled with hate, slander, accusations and a new list of demands about what you need to fix. For some of us, there is something inside that believes their lies about who you are—as a person, a parent, a partner, a friend, or a colleague.

The battle is relentless, wearing, and overwhelming.

Why do we give our co-parent so much credit? Why do we believe their lies about who we are rather than trusting our knowledge about who we are? When did our definition of ourselves become how they defined us?

Part of what makes an HCP so corruptly manipulative is their unique ability to build people up. To tell people exactly what they want to hear. To use existing insecurities to make them feel special. Once someone feels like their insecurities are special, they start to feel like anything is possible.

That's how some HCPs starts their path of control over you. They make you feel special by easing your insecurities, then make you feel like you need them to feel special. Then they start chipping away at you, saying if you could just fix yourself you could feel special again. And just like that, you spiral back into the old feelings and actions again.

CO-DEPENDENT: believing that your self-worth as a human is contingent on another person's acceptance of you.

If this sounds like you, your response pattern might be to believe that if you could just fix A, B or C about yourself, your life would be better. We all have room for improvement but it's time to remember who you are and the strengths you have.

"YOU WILL CONTINUE TO SUFFER IF YOU HAVE AN EMOTIONAL REACTION TO EVERYTHING THAT IS SAID TO YOU. TRUE POWER IS SITTING BACK AND OBSERVING EVERYTHING WITH LOGIC. IF WORDS CONTROL YOU THAT MEANS EVERYONE ELSE CAN CONTROL YOU. BREATHE AND ALLOW THINGS TO PASS."

– BRUCE LEE

FEELINGS TO MOVE
- ☐ Shame
- ☐ Guilt

QUESTIONS
1. What response patterns are you currently aware of?
2. How have they kept you safe?
3. What have they kept you safe from?

CHALLENGE
Think about the response patterns you have created. Write them down and don't beat yourself up over them.

TAKE CARE CHECKLIST
- ☐ How much sleep are you getting?
- ☐ How often do you get into nature?
- ☐ Have you taken a bath, Jacuzzi or sauna?
- ☐ Have you completed the Trigger Challenge?
- ☐ Are you spending time with friends?
- ☐ When was the last time you read a book for pleasure?
- ☐ Have you taken a walk recently?
- ☐ How often do you move your body?
- ☐ Are you eating well?
- ☐ Do you mediate? Yoga?

UNTIL'ISMS

Do you tell yourself that you can't do something until
_____ happens? You can't go on vacation with the
kids until the conflict with your co-parent settles...

...you can't move forward with quitting your job and starting your own business until you have a parenting plan order in place. You can't enter a new relationship until your co-parent agrees to the school schedule. You can't close this chapter to start a new chapter until your divorce is final.

THE COMMON WORD THROUGHOUT? "UNTIL"

You get stuck in this bizarre pattern where you think that once everything is settled and final that your life will go on. That you'll be able to live again, to be happy again, to go out again, to breathe again, to be a better parent again.

That you can't do all that until the tornado that is your life slows down. The most common words used to describe high-conflict co-parenting are chaos and exhaustion. You crave structure, follow-through and peace. You need sleep, lots and lots of sleep.

You are trying. Your until-isms aren't for a lack of trying. You are trying to put together a parenting plan that works for everyone, but each time you do it's only rejected and criticized with no other realistic options put forward by your co-parent. So, you put your life on hold until you have a plan that's agreed upon by everyone. Hoping that that day isn't too far off while suspecting or even knowing deep down inside that day is never going to come.

You've put your life on hold. Your joy. Your freedom. Your calm. You are waiting until your co-parent changes, until the courts change, until, until, until.

WAKE UP CALL: waiting until something happens, until something changes is a response pattern.

Until'isms keep you stuck in the quick-hardening cement. They keep you engaged in the conflict.

Until'isms keep you exactly where your high-conflict co-parent wants you—under their thumb.

Because while you are waiting until the conflict ends, your high-conflict co-parent isn't waiting. HCPs aren't programmed to live without the conflict, so it will never end for them. It. Will. Never. End. This is the HCP's operating system. It is hard-wired and will not change because you are nicer, neater, quieter, louder, more attractive, or thinner. But just because it will not end for them does not mean that you cannot change how you manage the relationship.

But how is an until'ism a response pattern? It's easy. Until'isms are easy.

Living, breathing, laughing and freedom are scary because the last time you experienced those feelings you got yourself into this mess. So, you put your life on hold until the conflict is over so you can rebuild, so you can learn to trust yourself and experience enjoyable feelings again. It's easier to wait until because it's safer. Then you realize one day that an entire decade has passed and you haven't progressed very far. That's okay. It's never too late to get over until-isms.

The key is acceptance and adjustment. Accept that you have a different experience from other parents and one that requires special handling that requires you to make the adjustments.

As soon as you utter the word until, ask yourself what you're waiting for. The conflict will never end so waiting for it to end is futile.

You owe it to yourself and your children to stop waiting until. Start living, laughing, breathing and feeling freedom today.

> **"AND IF THERE IS ONE THING YOU SHOULD DO, IT'S STOP BEING A PARADOX. YOU SAY YOU WANT TO BE HAPPY, YET YOU ALLOW YOURSELF TO BE SURROUNDED BY NEGATIVE PEOPLE. YOU SAY IT'S TIME FOR CHANGE, BUT THINGS STAY EXACTLY THE WAY THEY ALWAYS WERE. IT'S TIME TO BE EXACTLY THE PERSON YOU'VE ALWAYS WANTED TO BE. IT'S TIME TO TAKE CONTROL. IT'S TIME YOU LET YOURSELF BE HAPPY, BECAUSE MY GOODNESS, YOU DESERVE IT."**
>
> —UNKNOWN

FEELINGS TO MOVE
- ☐ Fear
- ☐ Worry

QUESTIONS
1. What until'isms have you put into place?
2. How are the until'isms keeping you safe?
3. If you waved a magic want and your co-parent conflict ended, what is the first thing you would do that you've been putting off?

CHALLENGE
This week we challenge you to get at least one until'ism off your list. Write down which one it is.

TAKE CARE CHECKLIST
- ☐ How much sleep are you getting?
- ☐ How often do you get into nature?
- ☐ Have you taken a bath, Jacuzzi or sauna?
- ☐ Have you completed the Trigger Challenge?
- ☐ Are you spending time with friends?
- ☐ When was the last time you read a book for pleasure?
- ☐ Have you taken a walk recently?
- ☐ How often do you move your body?
- ☐ Are you eating well?
- ☐ Do you mediate? Yoga?

"I'M IN A HURRY"

There is an old country song by the group, Alabama, with lyrics about being in a hurry to get things done and doing it so quickly that life loses its joy but with no reasonable explanation as to why we do it.

When the manic nature of your high-conflict co-parent erupts, you probably feel like you run and run and don't know why. You run and run because you're hopeful that maybe, just maybe, this time if you do everything they ask, they won't completely go off the deep end. You run and run because you are terrified of what might happen if you don't.

You run and run because you are trying to stay on top of the conflict, trying to predict what they may want or say or do so you sacrifice and you juggle forty-five different balls in an attempt to... attempt to what?

You run and run because you don't know what else to do.

And while you're running and running, what is your co-parent doing? Nothing. Except creating little fires everywhere. Pressuring you to put them out. So, while you run and run, they sit comfortably in their zone, acting on their impulses and recurring patterns of behavior. Huh?

Your comfort zone is a calm and peaceful place where people can rationally navigate their conflict, have a conversation, and move on.

Your high-conflict co-parents' comfort zone is when you are spiraling out-of-control because of all the fires they have lit for you to manage.

Your heartbeat increases during conflict, or even at the thought of seeing them. Your mind may go blank. Your co-parents' heartbeat may slow down during conflict or it may speed up. Either way, because they operate from an all-or-nothing mindset, their mind is very clear during that conflict, although it may not be logical.

SO, HOW IS RUNNING AND RUNNING A RESPONSE PATTERN?

Running and running is a fear of what will happen if you stop running. Your brain has created a pattern for you to cope with the crazy-making that is currently your life. It keeps you running and running with no formal destination. You become a hamster on a wheel, chasing and chasing. But chasing what? Chasing the mental and emotional peace you have decided is on the other side of running and running.

Are you in a hurry to get things done? You probably are, but the co-parenting conflict will never be done, no matter how far you run and run.

If you stop running and running, nothing will change in your co-parenting conflict except for a few extra fires that you may need to watch burn while your co-parent adjusts to your new personal thriving pattern.

FEELINGS TO MOVE

- ☐ Fear
- ☐ Worry
- ☐ Overexcitement

QUESTIONS

1. What feeling are you avoiding by rushing to get things done?
2. What would happen if nothing on your list got done?
3. Who benefits from you rushing?

CHALLENGE

This week we challenge you to catch yourself each time you feel the need to rush and rush. Instead of continuing to rush, take three slow deep breaths with your eyes closed.

TAKE CARE CHECKLIST

- ☐ How much sleep are you getting?
- ☐ How often do you get into nature?
- ☐ Have you taken a bath, Jacuzzi or sauna?
- ☐ Have you completed the Trigger Challenge?
- ☐ Are you spending time with friends?
- ☐ When was the last time you read a book for pleasure?
- ☐ Have you taken a walk recently?
- ☐ How often do you move your body?
- ☐ Are you eating well?
- ☐ Do you mediate? Yoga?

NOTE: we said "watch burn", not manage. That's important.

Remember that the issue isn't the issue. Once one issue is resolved there will always be a new issue. That's how they operate. So the choice is yours. March to the beat of their drum, or march to the beat of your own drum, managing your own emotions, behaviors and actions.

The lyrics in the old Alabama song continue about the voice in our heads that tells us we're running behind and better pick up the pace because it's a race, and goes a step further by saying second place isn't where you want to be.

When you stop listening to response pattern voices in your head and do the work to create thriving patterns instead, peace and freedom will find you.

"WHEN YOU GET REACTIVE, GET CURIOUS. YOU HAVE A WOUND THAT IS ASKING TO BE HEALED."

—MARK GROVES

PROGRESS CHECK-IN

TAKING CARE OF ME

3 ACTIVITIES outside my norm that improved my mood

1. _____

2. _____

3. _____

IMPROVING MY CO-PARENTING

3 STEPS I took to improve my co-parenting situation

1. _____

2. _____

3. _____

PROGRESS TO MAKE

1 SITUATION in which I could have done better with my co-parent or my kids

_____

_____

_____

MY SUCESSES

1 SITUATION I did well and I'm proud of

_____

_____

_____

REMINDERS

- ☐ Didn't take my frustration out on my kids
- ☐ Said something positive to my kids about their other parent, new partner, or grandparents (other family)
- ☐ Didn't yell at my kids
- ☐ BIFF'D all my written messages before sending them to my co-parent
- ☐ Reminded myself that I've got this!
- ☐ Reminded myself daily that I'm the only one who can manage my own emotions and behaviors

GOALS FOR NEXT MONTH

MY JOURNAL

SIDE EFFECTS

What does high-conflict co-parenting feel like?
Suffocation. Rage. Terror. Devastation. Bewilderment.
Sadness. Insanity producing. Humiliation. Self-doubt.
Frustration. Hopeless.

WHAT DOES IT LOOK LIKE?

Sleepless nights. Exhausted days. Short fuse. Lashing out. Lack of productivity at work and at home. Nail biting. Over-eating. Under-eating. Alcohol. Weed. Over-exercising. No exercise. Isolating.

Those are the glaringly obvious side effects of high-conflict co-parenting. But what about the subtle nuances that you don't realize are taking place? Like being mis-trustful of everyone you meet, creating a lack of connection with others for fear of getting conned again. Or being unsure of what you knew in the past about people. Who did I trust that I shouldn't have trusted? What did I miss? Am I stupid? Overly flawed? How can I ever trust myself again?

A voice inside your head that believes, sometimes for a split second and sometimes for hours, days, months, years that the horrible words and actions directed at you are true. A belief that this is all your fault. You should have been smarter, more aware, more turned in.

An underlying vibrational energy and mindset that you are forever screwing up your children. That you did this to them. That you are to blame for any horrible feelings your kids may feel at any given time.

A reoccurring cold, strep throat, pneumonia that you just can't shake. (You might want to read When the Body Says No: Understanding the Stress-Disease Connection by Gabor Maté, M.D.)

That anxious jump when you hear or see a new text or email has arrived, secretly paralyzing you for fear it might be your co-parent. And the ensuing mental gymnastics that keep you trying to fix whatever fire was just put to you rather than being present with your kids, your job, your friends and family.

The toll that co-parenting with someone high-conflict is far-reaching.

The thought patterns we have created and the feelings we feel around our self-worth, what we need to do to protect our children and our high-conflict co-parent become our response patterns. Our 'go to' reaction for a, b or c regardless if it has worked for us in the past or not. (It likely hasn't, but the reaction has become an unconscious response pattern. It's time to make those patterns conscious because once you're conscious you can start to shift from unconscious to awesome—regardless of what crazy-making is sent your way).

Consider this quote by **Geneen Roth:**

"ARE YOU BREATHING A LITTLE AND CALLING IT A LIFE?"

Eeks. I bet that hit home, didn't it?
Read it again.

You and your kids deserve at least once parent who is present, mentally strong, emotionally connected and mirroring the behaviors you one day hope your kids will use in their life when conflict arises.

This week we're going to dig deep to get at those hidden response patterns we shoved so far down we may not even know they are there. And what their side effects are.

"DON'T BURN YOUR OPPORTUNITIES FOR TEMPORARY COMFORT."

—UNKNOWN

FEELINGS TO MOVE

- ☐ Fear
- ☐ Anger
- ☐ Worry
- ☐ Grief

QUESTIONS

1. What would your life look like if you weren't co-parenting with who your co-parent?
2. How would you communicate differently?
3. What is stopping you from living that life? (Note: It's the story you are telling yourself)

CHALLENGE

This week we ask that you start a list of all the ill side-effects you are experiencing as a result of how you are currently managing your co-parenting conflict.

TAKE CARE CHECKLIST

- ☐ How much sleep are you getting?
- ☐ How often do you get into nature?
- ☐ Have you taken a bath, Jacuzzi or sauna?
- ☐ Have you completed the Trigger Challenge?
- ☐ Are you spending time with friends?
- ☐ When was the last time you read a book for pleasure?
- ☐ Have you taken a walk recently?
- ☐ How often do you move your body?
- ☐ Are you eating well?
- ☐ Do you mediate? Yoga?

PERFECT

It's the weirdest thing. Co-parenting has become something people have to do perfectly. Considering perfect doesn't exist, when did perfect parenting become an expectation?

WHAT DOES IT LOOK LIKE?

The expectation that kids need the:

- perfect parenting schedule
- perfect dietary food plan
- perfect school
- perfect doctor
- perfect outfit
- perfect haircut

The perfect haircut?

Yes. It's apparently a thing (eye roll).

And because perfect doesn't exist, you can never achieve it. This can only result in providing your high-conflict co-parent more ammunition to criticize your parenting skills and to berate them endlessly. You are often reminded just how imperfect you are.

Deep down you know perfect parenting isn't a reality or attainable by anyone, but in a continuous attempt to reduce the horrific ridicule, you have created a response pattern of trying to be the perfect parent.

You try to say the right thing. Do the right thing. Plan the right thing. Respond perfectly. Hold your temper perfectly. Discipline your kids perfectly.

You are on a continuous marry-go-round of trying to be perfect to stave off your co-parent's attacks while quietly criticizing yourself for not being able to be more perfect.

Awesome. Now both you and your co-parent are being mean to you. Think about that for a minute. You've begun to believe that you need to be perfect and in that believe alone you've crossed a line of trying to attain something unattainable.

When you co-parenting with an HCP, nothing you say, do, or plan will be the right thing, the perfect thing.

You could give your co-parent everything they asked for, every last request, and they would still find something wrong with your parenting, (and your family, your friends, your job, you... you get the point).

You have created a response pattern of striving for perfection in your parenting. When perfection isn't reached (and it will never be reached), your inner critic starts to validate your high-conflict co-parents' loud and relentless criticisms of your parenting.

Then you start to doubt yourself and your parenting skills, believing if you could just do x, y or z perfectly that the conflict might subside. But it's a repeated strategy of failure. Each time that logic fails you, your disappointment in yourself for not being perfect escalates and your resentment towards your co-parent for forcing you to be perfect increases tenfold.

FEELINGS TO MOVE

- ☐ Fear
- ☐ Worry

> ## "PARENTING ISN'T DOING. PARENTING IS PRESENCE. MENTALLY, PHYSICALLY AND EMOTIONALLY."
>
> —A.L.

But you've been brainwashed to believe you need to DO more, BE better, ACHIEVE greater, DISCIPLINE appropriately and SCHEDLULE perfectly in order to be the perfect parent.

Your kids don't need you to solve all their problems—they need you to teach them how to solve their own problems.

Kids don't need you to protect them from uncomfortable feelings, they need you to love them unconditionally while they move through those uncomfortable feelings, without judgement.

This week you're going to work towards a mindset of present parenting instead of *perfect parenting*.

> ## "IF A PERSON ALWAYS LEAVES YOU WITH MIXED FEELINGS, UNCERTAINTY AND AN UNSETTLED MIND, YOU DON'T NEED TO PLACE YOUR ENERGY THERE."
>
> —UNKNOWN

QUESTIONS

1. In what areas of your parenting have you been trying to be perfect?
2. How can you be present for your kids?
3. What does that look like when you've been triggered?

CHALLENGE

What would your parenting look like if no one was judging you? Parent like that this week.

TAKE CARE CHECKLIST

- ☐ How much sleep are you getting?
- ☐ How often do you get into nature?
- ☐ Have you taken a bath, Jacuzzi or sauna?
- ☐ Have you completed the Trigger Challenge?
- ☐ Are you spending time with friends?
- ☐ When was the last time you read a book for pleasure?
- ☐ Have you taken a walk recently?
- ☐ How often do you move your body?
- ☐ Are you eating well?
- ☐ Do you mediate? Yoga?

UNFAIR

When you are co-parenting with someone with high-conflict tendencies, a common thought that can turn into a mindset is that it's just so unfair.

IT'S UNFAIR

your kids have to be co-parenting by someone who hates their other parent.

It's unfair you have to strategically maneuver the legal system to try to win.

It's unfair that no one can stop the abuse, the manipulations, the control.

It's unfair you can't see your kids every day.

It's unfair that you didn't want the divorce but you have to suffer the consequences.

It's unfair that your kids are told mean, horrific, untrue stories about you.

It's unfair that you have to be stoic and friendly to new people in your children's lives over whom you have no choice or influence.

It's unfair that you gathered up the strength to leave the abusive relationship, only to continue relive the abuse through emails, texts, exchanges, Facebook posts, and even through your kids.

AND YOU'RE RIGHT. IT'S ALL UNFAIR.

Horrifically unfair. But if you get caught in the response pattern of what is unfair in your situation, you give your power to injustice of everything that is unfair. You are giving your power to the external.

And your focus becomes how to prove how unfair your situation is—to your friends, family, mediator, psychologist, lawyer, and to the judge or court system. Believing that someone somewhere will be able to see the unfairness and make it right. Make it fair.

And if you are stuck in the response pattern how unfair your situation is, giving away your power to an external source, you will never find peace of mind. Your kids won't have a present parent and you'll always be searching rather than being. By focusing on everything that is unfair, you are losing precious time with your kids and sacrificing an inner calm for yourself.

Your situation is unfair. Without a shadow of a doubt it's unfair. No amount of worrying, strategizing, thinking or talking about how unfair your situation is going to change that. Your response pattern of believing how unfair your situation is forces you to stay in the vicious conflict cycle, further allowing your co-parent to control both you and your situation.

Focusing on what is unfair takes away your ability to find the good in the benign, the everyday. It takes away your ability to find the good in yourself.

WHAAAAAT?

When was the last time you gave some attention to the good within you? When was the last time you praised yourself for a job well done? When was the last time your inner critic kept quiet for over an hour? When was the last time you accepted a compliment? And believed it?

Focusing on what is unfair robs you of your ability to nurture yourself and puts the focus on your high-conflict co-parent. Which. Is. Exactly. What. They. Want. All of the positive focus on them and none on you. It's time to look at the response pattern of what is unfair because it's not working for you—it's just working for your co-parent.

> "DON'T SEEK,
> DON'T SEARCH,
> DON'T ASK,
> DON'T KNOCK,
> DON'T DEMAND
> —RELAX.
> IF YOU RELAX,
> IT COMES.
> IF YOU RELAX,
> IT IS THERE.
> IF YOU RELAX,
> YOU START
> VIBRATING
> WITH IT."
> — OSHO

QUESTIONS

1. What do you find unfair about your current co-parenting relationship?
2. How could you shift your focus from unfair to finding the good in the benign, everyday minutia?
3. How do you find the good in your life?

CHALLENGE

This week, find a friend/professional who you will allow you to vent and then challenge you to find the good.

TAKE CARE CHECKLIST

- [ ] How much sleep are you getting?
- [ ] How often do you get into nature?
- [ ] Have you taken a bath, Jacuzzi or sauna?
- [ ] Have you completed the Trigger Challenge?
- [ ] Are you spending time with friends?
- [ ] When was the last time you read a book for pleasure?
- [ ] Have you taken a walk recently?
- [ ] How often do you move your body?
- [ ] Are you eating well?
- [ ] Do you mediate? Yoga?

WHAT IF

It's the monkey gymnastics your brain plays with you every day, or maybe every hour or minute. Most likely every minute.

What if my lawyer and I had made different decisions? Would my current situation been different?

What if I had never had kids with this person? What would my life look like?

What if my kids are forever screwed up because I couldn't save them from the other parent's high-conflict behaviors?

What if my kids end up hating me or turning against me because of the other parent's influence?

What if I get it wrong?

If you are what if'ing, then you are living in an imaginary place somewhere in the past or somewhere in the future, neither of which are good.

What if'ing the past breeds guilt and shame for the choices and decisions you have made and how they affect the ones you love most. It gives credit to regret.

What if'ing the future also breeds guilt and shame but instead of regret, what if'ing the future romanticizes hope. Hope that your co-parent will change. Hope that you aren't screwing up your kids. Hope that someone, somewhere will understand what you're going through and help fix it.

What if'ing the past contributes to depression, and what if'ing the future is a slippery slope into anxiety.

Other than the obvious, what if'ing is dangerous for another more primary reason. Rarely do people what if themselves into unconditional love of self, non-judgement of self, self-acceptance. No, what if'ing always involves external measures to be changed. External circumstances. External relations.

If your response pattern is what if'ing, you are either trying to fix a past that can't be fixed or trying to control a future that can't be controlled. If you're in the past or future, you aren't in the present, so you're not being the best you for yourself or for your kids.

You may be asking yourself how you can strategize your next steps if you don't go through every what if future scenario? There is a time and place for legal strategy and for developing a plan for moving forward. Be honest with yourself—that isn't what you're what if'ing. It may start out that way. Your first thought may be strategy-related but within 5-10 minutes you've been sucked into the what if vortex of guilt, shame, regret and hope for a past or future you can't control. And not once did these thoughts cross your mind:

- What if I just loved myself?
- What if I put myself first?
- What if I made nurturing myself part of my daily routine?

Sounds blasphemous, but it's true. When was the last time you were nice to yourself? Mind, body and/or spirit?

Your what if response pattern is keeping you safe from the scariest feeling of all—unconditional love for yourself. Because loving yourself is selfish and takes too much precious time. You've convinced yourself that you aren't worthy. Think about it: do these sound like your high-conflict co-parent's words or your words?

Start paying attention to the tape playing in your head and notice how many external what if's you play with in a day and how many revolve around self-compassion versus self-hate.

"YOU WILL NEVER GET THE TRUTH OUT OF A NARCISSIST. THE CLOSEST YOU WILL EVER COME IS A STORY THAT EITHER MAKES THEM THE VICTIM OR THE HERO, BUT NEVER THE VILLAIN."

–SHANNON L. ALDER

FEELINGS TO MOVE

☐ Fear
☐ Worry
☐ Anger

QUESTIONS

1. What could your brain focus on if you weren't constantly questioning what if?
2. What activities could you be spending your time doing if you weren't asking what if?
3. What are your what ifs?

CHALLENGE

This week when you catch yourself focusing on what if, shift your thinking to what is. Laugh, and then go do something distracting.

TAKE CARE CHECKLIST

☐ How much sleep are you getting?
☐ How often do you get into nature?
☐ Have you taken a bath, Jacuzzi or sauna?
☐ Have you completed the Trigger Challenge?
☐ Are you spending time with friends?
☐ When was the last time you read a book for pleasure?
☐ Have you taken a walk recently?
☐ How often do you move your body?
☐ Are you eating well?
☐ Do you mediate? Yoga?

PROGRESS CHECK-IN

TAKING CARE OF ME

3 ACTIVITIES outside my norm that improved my mood

1. _____

2. _____

3. _____

IMPROVING MY CO-PARENTING

3 STEPS I took to improve my co-parenting situation

1. _____

2. _____

3. _____

PROGRESS TO MAKE

1 SITUATION in which I could have done better with my co-parent or my kids

_____

_____

MY SUCESSES

1 SITUATION I did well and I'm proud of

_____

_____

REMINDERS

☐ Didn't take my frustration out on my kids

☐ Said something positive to my kids about their other parent, new partner, or grandparents (other family)

☐ Didn't yell at my kids

☐ BIFF'D all my written messages before sending them to my co-parent

☐ Reminded myself that I've got this!

☐ Reminded myself daily that I'm the only one who can manage my own emotions and behaviors

GOALS FOR NEXT MONTH

MY JOURNAL

INDECISION

True or false? You are one decision away from a completely different life. True. But how do you know which decision to make? What if you make the wrong one? What if everything changes?
What if my decision makes everything worse?

Notice all the negative questions, expecting a poor outcome for whatever decision you make? Your internal dialogue, your response pattern, is a belief that no decision is easier than the possible fallout from the wrong decision. It's cliché to say that there is no wrong decision, but it's accurate. The only wrong decision is no decision.

Hovering in the purgatory of indecision? Having both feet firmly planted in two different canoes and the canoes are driving apart? It's the deluxe version of crazy-making. You, driving yourself super crazy. Like managing a high-conflict co-parent wasn't crazy-making enough, do you really need to add driving yourself crazy with indecision? No.

If you aren't making your own decisions then someone else is making them for you. And that someone is likely your controlling, manipulative co-parent. You might be thinking there are consequences for the decisions you make and you have to make sure you get it right!

WHAT ABOUT THE CONSEQUENCES FOR NOT MAKING A DECISION?

The indecision response pattern allows you to keep blaming someone or something else for what is happening in your life. If you make a decision, you'll have to suffer the consequences. But if you don't make a decision then you can keep blaming your co-parent for everything that's wrong with your parenting plan, your kids' behaviors, your life (or lack thereof).

What if you made a change from: If I make a decision, I'll have to suffer the consequences.

If I make a decision, I can start moving into possibility.

Being stuck in indecision keeps you doing what you've always done. Doing what you've always done hasn't worked for you—but it is familiar—and familiar is comfortable, safe, even if the safe and familiar don't feel good. They are at least feelings you know and know how to react to.

Response patterns are our go to reactions for anything that makes us feel outside our comfort zone or unsafe. It's our patterned reaction to the uncomfortable that is comfortable.

Example: prior to understanding my response patterns, I spent years thinking I was Jekyll and Hyde. I was a calm(ish), skilled mediator by day and a raging lunatic by night. My response pattern was rage and I had a razor-sharp trigger reaction. It took very little to set me off. Once I was raging it would take me days to recover. Exhaustion, guilt and shame for my reaction followed with a promise to myself that I would just utilize my daytime skills as a mediator for when I was triggered by the high-conflict person in my life. Until the next time I was triggered, a week or two later. I'd fall into my response pattern and rage out all my energy until exhaustion, guilt and shame started. REPEAT.

Having the confidence and faith in yourself to believe that whichever decision you make will be better than the response pattern of indecision is imperative not only to your co-parenting survival but also for taking back control of the possible outcome.

It's time to stop blaming your co-parent for the decisions that are being made without you while you are stuck in indecision.

> **"I'M VERY CAUTIOUS ABOUT WHO HAS ACCESS TO ME LATELY. AND IT'S NOT OUT OF ARROGANCE, IT'S OUT OF THE NEED TO CONTINUE TO PROTECT MY SPACE AND ENERGY AS I CONTINUE TO DO THE WORK TO ELEVATE MYSELF. THIS CHAPTER OF ME REQUIRES ME TO BE A LITTLE LESS ACCESSIBLE."**
> — UNKNOWN

FEELINGS TO MOVE
- ☐ Fear
- ☐ Worry

QUESTIONS
1. What areas of your life are you struggling in indecision?
2. What feeling is holding you back from making a decision?
3. What would happen if you made the wrong decision?

CHALLENGE
This week the challenge is to make 3 decisions—big or small—just make them.

TAKE CARE CHECKLIST
- ☐ How much sleep are you getting?
- ☐ How often do you get into nature?
- ☐ Have you taken a bath, Jacuzzi or sauna?
- ☐ Have you completed the Trigger Challenge?
- ☐ Are you spending time with friends?
- ☐ When was the last time you read a book for pleasure?
- ☐ Have you taken a walk recently?
- ☐ How often do you move your body?
- ☐ Are you eating well?
- ☐ Do you mediate? Yoga?

HATE
PART 1

Here's the thing about hate: it's an extreme emotion. What does that mean? What is an extreme emotion? Hate, similar to love, is a whole mind, body and spirit experience.

While love fills you with the greatest feelings you've ever had—elation, joy, bliss, confidence, possibility. Hate fills you with the worst feelings you've ever had—black-out rage, aggression, unimaginable thoughts of creating pain or misery for someone else. Hate makes you feel vindictive, revengeful and bitter.

Love and hate are on the same spectrum. They may have very different internal reactions and present as opposites, but they are both extreme emotions. When we are in an extreme emotion, we are rarely (never) rational. Or present. Or communicating clearly. Or making good decisions.

WE ARE EITHER DRUNK ON LOVE OR HIGH ON HATE.

Drunk on love? High on hate? When you've been triggered, your endorphins spike, making you temporarily impaired. Your endorphins don't know the difference between love and hate—they just know they've been activated, so they jump into action and make you temporarily impaired—good or bad. Stick with me here.

If your response pattern is hate, your response pattern is the high that is created when you are triggered. It's not a good high. It's more like a bad trip or an overdose, but it's a high nonetheless. It's a huge release of endorphins with nowhere to go but out. How do those endorphins show up? In feelings of rage, seething contempt, and jaw-clenching fury.

You may not like those feelings but they seem to be working for you. Feeling hate gives you permission to defend yourself, encourages you to react to the lies and manipulations, and tricks you into thinking your behavior is justified.

But hate is keeping you engaged in the conflict. When you're engaged in the conflict you are giving your power to your co-parent because while you're raging, with a heartbeat of 140 beats per minute, your co-parent is calmly sitting back and enjoying the fruits of their hate-inducing labor (some people with on the higher end of the high-conflict spectrum react to conflict differently than those who don't have high-conflict tendencies—their heartbeats don't race in the face of conflict; instead, they slow down).

Your goal is to shift your hate response pattern to a state of disengagement. When you no longer hate your co-parent, you take back the power to control your emotions—good and bad—and when you can effectively manage your emotions in the face of conflict, you'll find genuine inner peace.

FEELINGS TO MOVE

- ☐ Anger
- ☐ Fear
- ☐ Worry
- ☐ Grief

QUESTIONS

1. In what circumstances do you feel hate?
2. How does the feeling of hate affect you physically?
3. Who has the power to trigger you into hate?

CHALLENGE

This week, your challenge is to observe what happens to you when you feel hate. Get curious about the different sensations happening in your brain and your body.

TAKE CARE CHECKLIST

- ☐ How much sleep are you getting?
- ☐ How often do you get into nature?
- ☐ Have you taken a bath, Jacuzzi or sauna?
- ☐ Have you completed the Trigger Challenge?
- ☐ Are you spending time with friends?
- ☐ When was the last time you read a book for pleasure?
- ☐ Have you taken a walk recently?
- ☐ How often do you move your body?
- ☐ Are you eating well?
- ☐ Do you mediate? Yoga?

"INSANITY IS WHEN YOU LOVE SOMEONE SO MUCH, YOU HELP THEM DESTROY YOU BY TRYING TO SAVE THEM."

—UNKNOWN

WEEK 11

HATE
PART 2

While you may think that all your hate is aimed at your co-parent, the likelihood that your hate is also self-directed is pretty high.
We could likely say that it is guaranteed.

If you are co-parenting with someone who is high-conflict, take a moment and reflect how many times you've asked yourself:

- How could I be so stupid?
- What was I thinking?
- What is wrong with me that I missed the signs?
- How will my kids ever forgive me?

All questions that indicate a level of self-judgement. Self-judgement equals self-hatred. Have you ever said this to yourself:

- But I wouldn't hate myself if I hadn't had kids with such a mean person.
- But I wouldn't judge my decisions if we could just be amicable.
- But I am taking responsibility for my actions, I am to blame for this mess. I had kids with a monster.

You can have all the buts you want, but self-hate didn't just start with this relationship. Self-hate isn't new to you. It's just been put under a magnifying glass with this particular experience you're having.

It was your underlying response pattern of self-hate that allowed you to be vulnerable to someone (your co-parent) who told you how special you were, who built you up, who seemed to love you despite all your perceived flaws. And damn, that felt awesome.

Because if you had known how special you were, how loveable you were, then feeling special and loved by someone else wouldn't have been so intoxicating.

You fell under the spell of your high-conflict co-parent and all of their charms because secretly you felt like you didn't measure up. Finding a romantic partner who believed in you more than you believed in yourself suddenly started to make you feel like maybe you weren't so bad after all—that maybe you were lovable. You started to stand a little taller and strut a little more confidently. You felt powerful, strong, loved. Just not by the right person.

You were susceptible to the charms and manipulations of your high-conflict co-parent because they helped you feel about yourself that you should have been able to feel without their help.

And because that self-hate was still lingering under the surface of falling in love, when their charms turned to criticisms, a little tiny piece of you believed their criticisms to be true and then you started saying to yourself:

- Maybe I'm not that great at my job.
- Maybe I'm not a good parent.
- Maybe my past has made me less worthy of happiness.
- Maybe I am crazy.

FEELINGS TO MOVE

☐ Anger
☐ Fear
☐ Worry
☐ Grief

Without the response pattern of self-hate sitting quietly in the background, your co-parent's criticisms wouldn't have created that doubt inside your head. Your co-parents' words and actions wouldn't have cut you off at the knees and put you in a position of hating yourself even more.

Self-hate is like venom that will kill you. It's just a matter of how strong the venom is. The antidote? Self-acceptance, regardless of your flaws. Non-self-judgement, regardless of your mistakes. Self-love, regardless of other people's opinions.

QUESTIONS

1. What does hating yourself feel like?
2. What prompts you to feel that way about yourself?
3. What would the opposite of self-hate look like?

CHALLENGE

This week we challenge you to snap your fingers each time a self-hate or self-loathing thought pops into your head.

"THE MORE YOU LOVE YOUR DECISIONS, THE LESS YOU NEED OTHERS TO LOVE THEM."
—UNKNOWN

TAKE CARE CHECKLIST

☐ How much sleep are you getting?
☐ How often do you get into nature?
☐ Have you taken a bath, Jacuzzi or sauna?
☐ Have you completed the Trigger Challenge?
☐ Are you spending time with friends?
☐ When was the last time you read a book for pleasure?
☐ Have you taken a walk recently?
☐ How often do you move your body?
☐ Are you eating well?
☐ Do you mediate? Yoga?

EXHALE

How often do you find yourself clenching your jaw? Fisting your palms? Squeezing your shoulders to your ears? Holding your breath? Curling your toes? Furrowing your brow? Popping pain killers for a headache? Or all of the above? All at once?

Being stuck in your current circumstances creates a level of physical stress on our bodies that we tend to ignore. Rather, we subconsciously know it's there, but we just don't know what to do about it. So we choose to ignore it.

But at what cost? To ourselves and our children?

Elevated levels of stress have been linked to a litany of health challenges such as heart problems, anxiety, depression, forgetfulness and exhaustion. Stress can also present itself as strep throat, pneumonia, migraines and sore joints. Wrinkles, sore feet and an upset stomach.

If you are co-parenting with someone who has high-conflict tendencies, your stress levels will be high—ridiculously high. And if your response pattern has been to hold all your feelings, all your stress, all your everything in your body rather than feel the discomfort of the present moment in your current situation, then it's time to exhale. But you won't, because if you allow yourself exhale and feel all that you need to feel, you might fall apart. You don't have time to fall apart or become more vulnerable. Your co-parent might use it against you.

AH! TOO MUCH INFORMATION. LET'S BREAK IT DOWN.

You have created a response pattern of inhaling and holding. And holding. And holding. Holding your breath, holding your body rigidly, holding on. If you keep holding on, then you don't have to fully face your sadness, your heartbreak, your disappointment in your current circumstances. Holding on to hope that a unicorn might gallop in and sprinkle pixie dust to make your co-parent easier to manage.

But you can only hold on for so long until your body forces you to exhale. Forces you to surrender and accept that you will never have a white picket fence co-parenting relationship and your co-parent will never be nice regardless of how many fires you put out.

Instead of waiting for your body to force you to exhale, take control of your breath now. Exhale your shoulders, your brow, your fists. Exhale your clenched jaw, your toes and your breath.

Just sit. Sit in whatever discomfort arises. Inhale. Exhale.

Trust me, you won't break. You may cry a mountain of tears, but you won't break.

Exhale.

FEELINGS TO MOVE
- ☐ Fear
- ☐ Worry
- ☐ Grief

QUESTIONS
1. What are you hoping your unicorn will do for you?
2. What and how are you holding in your life?
3. What would exhaling look like to you?

CHALLENGE
This week we challenge you to notice when you're holding on—physically, emotionally, mentally—and catch yourself. When you sense you are holding on—exhale. One, great big, noisy exhale.

TAKE CARE CHECKLIST
- ☐ How much sleep are you getting?
- ☐ How often do you get into nature?
- ☐ Have you taken a bath, Jacuzzi or sauna?
- ☐ Have you completed the Trigger Challenge?
- ☐ Are you spending time with friends?
- ☐ When was the last time you read a book for pleasure?
- ☐ Have you taken a walk recently?
- ☐ How often do you move your body?
- ☐ Are you eating well?
- ☐ Do you mediate? Yoga?

"DON'T LET YOUR MIND BULLY YOUR BODY INTO BELIEVING IT HAS TO CARRY THE BURDEN OF ITS WORRIES."
—ASTRID ALAUDA

"YOUR RELATIONSHIP WITH YOURSELF SETS THE TONE FOR EVERY OTHER RELATIONSHIP YOU HAVE."
—UNKNOWN

PROGRESS CHECK-IN

TAKING CARE OF ME

3 ACTIVITIES outside my norm that improved my mood

1. ....
2. ....
3. ....

IMPROVING MY CO-PARENTING

3 STEPS I took to improve my co-parenting situation

1. ....
2. ....
3. ....

PROGRESS TO MAKE

1 SITUATION in which I could have done better with my co-parent or my kids

....

....

....

MY SUCESSES

1 SITUATION I did well and I'm proud of

....

....

....

REMINDERS

☐ Didn't take my frustration out on my kids

☐ Said something positive to my kids about their other parent, new partner, or grandparents (other family)

☐ Didn't yell at my kids

☐ BIFF'D all my written messages before sending them to my co-parent

☐ Reminded myself that I've got this!

☐ Reminded myself daily that I'm the only one who can manage my own emotions and behaviors

GOALS FOR NEXT MONTH

MY JOURNAL

PARALYZED

Do you find yourself waking up at 3 a.m. drafting emails to your co-parent? Re-writing them in your brain. Over and over? Imagining their response to each slight change you make to the draft you can't quite get right?

Where did this bizarre anxiety come from? You never used to be afraid to send emails. When did you suddenly start overthinking each word? How do you stop being so afraid to hit the send button?

Communicating with someone who has high-conflict tendencies isn't just scary, intimidating and anxiety-producing. It's so much more than feeling anxious about hitting send. It's a level of terror that no one else seems to understand.

Your friends and family think you should just get over it, say what you need to say and hit send. But they don't fully understand the complexities of the response you're going to get. They don't understand that if your email isn't perfect, you'll be hit with 100 passive aggressive criticisms instead of just 50 and your emotional state just can't take one more email filled with put downs, lies, manipulations and cruelty.

So, you find yourself paralyzed at 3 a.m. drafting email response in your head, trying to get it perfect. Trying to figure out a way to stop the abusive email you're going to get in response to anything and everything you say, regardless of how perfectly it's worded.

What your brain is forgetting to tell you, because it's paralyzed in an anxiety attack, is that it doesn't really matter what is in your email—your co-parent is going to attack you.

READ THAT AGAIN: It doesn't really matter what is in your email—your co-parent is going to attack you.

But you want to make sure that if a judge one day reads the emails you look like the calm and flexible parent? To look like the calm and flexible parent, you have to be the calm and flexible parent.

Novel concept! How is it possible to be the calm and flexible parent when you're paralyzed by fear of an email response? Recognize your response pattern and then do the work to shift it.

If being paralyzed in fear or terror has you awake at 3 a.m. drafting perfect emails to your co-parent in your head, with the goal of not getting a mean and nasty response back, then you are continuing to give away your power to someone/something that can't be controlled.

Your emails should be 4 sentences or less and contain no insight, no emotional words and no opinion. Refrain from using the word "I" unless you using it the sentence "I propose".

You need sleep. Let's shift your pattern from paralyzed anxiety to calm and flexible so you can be that person and not just try and look that way.

FEELINGS TO MOVE

- ☐ Fear
- ☐ Worry
- ☐ Grief

QUESTIONS

1. What is keeping you paralyzed? Be specific.
2. How has being paralyzed changed your life?
3. How has being paralyzed contributed to your co-parent continuing to have control and you continuing to be the victim?

CHALLENGE

This week we challenge you to get moving. Write, walk, clean, do jumping jacks. Do anything that requires movement to help you get unanalyzed.

TAKE CARE CHECKLIST

- ☐ How much sleep are you getting?
- ☐ How often do you get into nature?
- ☐ Have you taken a bath, Jacuzzi or sauna?
- ☐ Have you completed the Trigger Challenge?
- ☐ Are you spending time with friends?
- ☐ When was the last time you read a book for pleasure?
- ☐ Have you taken a walk recently?
- ☐ How often do you move your body?
- ☐ Are you eating well?
- ☐ Do you mediate? Yoga?

"COURAGE IS THE ABILITY TO HAVE FAITH, PERSISTENCE AND STRENGTH IN THE FACE OF FEAR, PAIN AND STRESS. HAVE FAITH TODAY. KEEP PERSISTING TOWARD YOUR DREAMS BECAUSE THE WORLD NEEDS YOU."

—BRENDON BURCHARD

CONTROL

Of course you feel the need to control. Your life feels totally out-of-control.

This isn't how you thought parenting would look—unable to even register your child for school without consent that you can't get because your co-parent disagrees with your choice—not because the school is bad but because the school was your idea.

Unable to travel without a consent to travel letter, which you can't get unless you apply to the courts because your co-parent won't grant permission. And agreeing on extra-curricular activities? As high-conflict expert, Bill Eddy, LCSW, Esq. says, "Fuhged-daboudit"

"WE FEEL THE NEED TO CONTROL WHEN WE FEEL OUT OF CONTROL."

—A.L.

You've lost the ability to make basic decisions for your children simply because you are no longer in an intact relationship with their other parent. You are under a microscope for everything you say and do and regardless of your intensions. Your words and actions are almost always twisted into something negative.

You feel like a puppet, being forced to comply with whatever the puppeteer wants.

And now you're done. You are done being on the wrong side of the control. You're done being told you don't know what is in your kid's best interest. You're done not being able to help shape your kids with your values and views. You're done feeing like nothing you say or do matters—that your co-parent gets everything they want and you don't.

So, you stick your heels in the sand and hit a full stop. Your life has come to a point where it feels so out-of-control that you decide to take back control of the situation because nothing else has worked. Except that it's not really control you want. What you want is mutual respect and decision-making. Being controlling isn't really your thing. You just know you can't live another second living under your co-parent's thumb.

But you're taking back control from your out-of-control life. So you start sending demanding emails; you start limiting parenting time; you start trying to control Christmas, Easter, summer holidays. It feels good at first. You're doing something to counter your co-parents control! You're standing up to your co-parent. You're using your voice! You're giving your kids a voice!

But that good feeling quickly passes because you realize that when you try to control, you are giving your co-parent the fight and the resistance they want. However, the conflict doesn't decrease, it escalates. You are no longer feeling in control, in fact, you're feeling even more out-of-control because not only are you losing the conflict battle, you are going against your core value system.

FEELINGS TO MOVE
☐ Fear
☐ Anger

If your response pattern is to control when you feel out-of-control, it's because you are trying to feel powerful in a powerless situation. Your situation feels powerless because you've given up your power, to an external source.

What you really want is to let go; let go of the fear, the anger, the sorrow, the resentment, the what ifs, the despair, the sadness, the loss of self, the anxiety and the control. Oddly enough, letting go of control will give you control. Let's unravel your control response pattern and get you to a more awesome place.

QUESTIONS
1. What aspects of your life are you trying to control?
2. What would it feel like to let go of that control?
3. What would your world look like if you let go of that control?

CHALLENGE
This week we challenge you to surrender one area of your life where you are hyper controlling it, because you feel out of control. Just one area. For just one week.

"THE ONLY PERSON I EVER LOST AND NEEDED BACK WAS MYSELF."
—UNKNOWN

TAKE CARE CHECKLIST
☐ How much sleep are you getting?
☐ How often do you get into nature?
☐ Have you taken a bath, Jacuzzi or sauna?
☐ Have you completed the Trigger Challenge?
☐ Are you spending time with friends?
☐ When was the last time you read a book for pleasure?
☐ Have you taken a walk recently?
☐ How often do you move your body?
☐ Are you eating well?
☐ Do you mediate? Yoga?

CHOCOLATE

When your world hits the proverbial fan, what do you reach for? Chips? Cheese? Wine? Do you vent? Exercise? Binge-watch Netflix?

Or do you reach for that velvety smooth, deliciously creamy chocolate you stash in the freezer you keep hoping you'll forget is there? (Did I just give away one of my response patterns?).

Everyone involved with a high-conflict co-parent has a go-to vice they use to check out of reality and to numb the insanity that has become their life. Most people refer to it as self-sabotage, a way of hurting themselves so they can't achieve what they want to achieve.

- Can't stick to a diet? Self-sabotage.
- Can't stick to a fitness program? Self-sabotage.
- Can't stay disengaged from your co-parent? Self-sabotage.

By calling it self-sabotage, you are condemning yourself for a pattern of behavior that was created (by you, probably unconsciously) to keep you feeling safe. If you're trying to keep you safe, is self-sabotage an accurate description of what you're doing?

Instead, let's call that go-to activity we do when our world becomes too much mentally and emotionally to manage, a response pattern we (probably unconsciously) created to keep us feeling safe. Self-sabotage continues the narrative that you are a bad person because you can't figure your life out. Response patterns allow you to examine why you (probably unconsciously) created them (to feel safe) without judgement nor self-criticism.

Self-sabotage becomes an identity, a response pattern is just a pattern. Once you are aware of your patterns, you change the patterns that are no longer working for you.

Self-sabotage example: Every time, and I mean every time I was triggered into my chocolate response pattern it would unfold like this. The high-conflict person would lie to me (my trigger) and I would get so angry and frustrated that my mind would go blank. If I didn't have chocolate in the house, I'd drive to the store and get it. Not just one chocolate bar—usually three. Because three made sense to me (keep in mind that we are not rational when we're triggered). I would eat all three chocolate bars on the way home, sometimes enjoying the deliciousness of the chocolate but more often than not, just inhaling the chocolate for the quick 10-minute sugar rush of distraction that followed. Once I was home, my inner self-critic would take over. "You're so stupid and you have no will power. You can't even control what you eat, how can you raise kids?" You get the point. It was self-judgement on steroids. It was ugly and mean and served its purpose. It reaffirmed that all of my co-parent's criticisms of me were true—I wasn't worthy. I was pathetic.

FEELINGS TO MOVE
- ☐ Fear
- ☐ Anger
- ☐ Worry
- ☐ Grief
- ☐ Over excitement

QUESTIONS
1. What numbing agent do you use to distract yourself from your trigger?
2. Has numbing kept you safe?
3. What new, non-numbing behavior can you do when triggered?

CHALLENGE
This week we challenge you to stock your fridge with celery and whenever your response pattern to inhale some chocolate kicks in, grab celery instead (or find a comparable challenge for your response pattern).

TAKE CARE CHECKLIST
- ☐ How much sleep are you getting?
- ☐ How often do you get into nature?
- ☐ Have you taken a bath, Jacuzzi or sauna?
- ☐ Have you completed the Trigger Challenge?
- ☐ Are you spending time with friends?
- ☐ When was the last time you read a book for pleasure?
- ☐ Have you taken a walk recently?
- ☐ How often do you move your body?
- ☐ Are you eating well?
- ☐ Do you mediate? Yoga?

Response pattern example: Now that I understand the difference between self-sabotage and response patterns designed to help me feel safe, I can see that my chocolate binging was a way to shut my brain off from all the external stress it was managing. The negative self-talk that followed was just allowing me to stay small, where I perceived safety to exist. It's so much safer to believe the lies we tell ourselves, the lies others tell us we are, than to dig a little deeper and discover the depths of our personality.

If your response pattern is chocolate (or some other numbing agent), it's time to let yourself off the hook—you're not self-sabotaging. Forgive yourself for trying to keep yourself feeling safe the only way you knew how. Start creating and re-wiring your brain in new directions.

"YOU DON'T ALWAYS NEED A PLAN. SOMETIMES YOU JUST NEED TO BREATHE. TRUST. LET GO. AND SEE WHAT HAPPENS."
—BREAKING FREE

EASY

Most people think leaving is going to be the hardest part. That once you were free from the abuse, the control and the manipulations, that you could start living again. That you would be free.

That you would be able to protect your kids from the horror that you had to experience. Now you're *out*. You mustered up all the courage and strength you had in you to leave, and you left. You did it.

But it's not easier. In fact, it's harder. At least when you were still in the relationship you saw your kids every day and had daily influence in their lives. You could plan their meals. You could help them through tough days at school.

Now? Now you have to send them off to spend time with someone you know isn't going to put the kids needs ahead of their own and someone you know will criticize you to try and win their love. Because in their minds the kids can't love you both—it has to be one or the other. They will do anything in their power to make sure the kids love them and not love you.

Now? Now you have to communicate even more with the person who spent years trying to destroy you. Email and email, text after text, trying to control you through lies and manipulations of the legal system rather than emotional freak-outs under your roof.

Sometimes… sometimes you think about what it would have been like if you'd just stayed. Maybe staying in the relationship and all the dramatic abuse would have been easier than having to send your kids off to a monster. At least when you were all under one roof, you could protect them just a little.

If your response pattern is to think about whether staying in the relationship would have been easier than having to co-parent apart, then you are still bartering with your present to change your past.

Staying wasn't an option. Staying was hell. Staying was sucking your soul one second at a time. You may be thinking that staying would have allowed you to spend more time with your kids. Staying also would have taught your kids that abuse is okay, that being co-dependent is okay, that relationships are about power and control, and you would have exposed them to damaging parental conflict.

Leaving, putting your safety and your well-being first, tells your kids it's okay to do the same. That they are worthy of more. You may be thinking you should have stayed because your kids are being abused by their other parent because you're not there to protect them.

Some say that your role as their parent isn't to save your kids—it's to give them the tools to protect themselves. However, this is a personal decision that should be made with the assistance of professionals who can help you explore safe options. Keep in mind that abuse is never okay and you should protect yourself and your kids.

Staying usually is not an option—it definitely was not for me. Romanticizing what could have been because it would have been *easier* will keep you from creating your next version of you.

"SOMETIMES HAVING COFFEE WITH YOUR BEST FRIEND, IS ALL THE THERAPY YOU NEED"

—UNKNOWN

FEELINGS TO MOVE

☐ Fear
☐ Anger
☐ Worry
☐ Grief
☐ Over excitement

QUESTIONS

1. How would your life look if it were easy?
2. How would you spend your time if life were easy?
3. What is making your life not easy?

CHALLENGE

This week we challenge you to do the things you would do if your life were easy.

TAKE CARE CHECKLIST

☐ How much sleep are you getting?
☐ How often do you get into nature?
☐ Have you taken a bath, Jacuzzi or sauna?
☐ Have you completed the Trigger Challenge?
☐ Are you spending time with friends?
☐ When was the last time you read a book for pleasure?
☐ Have you taken a walk recently?
☐ How often do you move your body?
☐ Are you eating well?
☐ Do you mediate? Yoga?

PROGRESS CHECK-IN

TAKING CARE OF ME
3 ACTIVITIES outside my norm
that improved my mood

1. _____

2. _____

3. _____

IMPROVING MY CO-PARENTING
3 STEPS I took to improve
my co-parenting situation

1. _____

2. _____

3. _____

PROGRESS TO MAKE
1 SITUATION in which I
could have done better with
my co-parent or my kids

_____

_____

_____

MY SUCESSES
1 SITUATION I did well
and I'm proud of

_____

_____

_____

REMINDERS
- ☐ Didn't take my frustration out on my kids
- ☐ Said something positive to my kids about their other
  parent, new partner, or grandparents (other family)
- ☐ Didn't yell at my kids
- ☐ BIFF'D all my written messages before
  sending them to my co-parent
- ☐ Reminded myself that I've got this!
- ☐ Reminded myself daily that I'm the only one
  who can manage my own emotions and behaviors

GOALS FOR NEXT MONTH

MY JOURNAL

MARTYR

A martyr is one who puts others needs ahead of their own to the detriment of oneself.

You might be thinking that doesn't apply to you. You might believe that you were putting yourself first when you left or you put your kid's other parent's needs ahead of your own because if you didn't, then he or she would make your life a living hell. Or how about the belief that you always put your mask on first?

Yet when an email or text from your high-conflict co-parent pop up on your phone and you break into a sweat or have a panic attack, not knowing what unrealistic demands and expectations may be placed on you today, your immediate response is to fix whatever complaint is being expressed. All in the hope that the demands won't escalate.

See my point?

Sometimes it feels easier just to fix whatever problem is presented to you (or yelled at you in email with ALL CAPS on) than to try and implement a boundary or disengage. Boundaries take work. They create more emotionally charged situations before they reduce them. They force you to put your needs ahead of anyone else's. That feels gross and uncomfortable!

DISENGAGING TAKES SCARY, TERRIFYING EFFORT.

So many what ifs pop up when you try to disengage like:

- "What if they take me to court because I didn't respond to their email?"
- "What if they get sole custody because I didn't change my travel plans to accommodate their last-minute right of first refusal request?"
- "What if they say really mean and awful things about me to our kids?"

What if? The what ifs are endless and possible. When you are co-parenting with someone who presents as high-conflict, anything is possible. What many fail to realize, because they are so fixated on trying to protect themselves from the what ifs, is that the what ifs are going to happen regardless whether or not you are disengaging from the conflict or creating boundaries to give yourself space to think and breathe.

You can't control the what ifs from happening. No amount of fixing (at the expense of your own well-being) will stop your high-conflict co-parent from acting out the worst-case what if scenario if that's the route they choose to take.

FEELINGS TO MOVE
- ☐ Anger
- ☐ Grief
- ☐ Fear
- ☐ Worry

If your response pattern is to be a martyr, to put your co-parent's demands and your children's needs ahead of your own, then it is time to start exploring your need to be liked. Acting like a martyr creates feelings of resentment, exhaustion, tension and bitterness. That's not you! You've just taken on a role, a response pattern, that you believed would keep you safe. And it worked (ish). But it's not working anymore because your self-worth knows that no amount of martyrdom is going to change this situation for you. No amount of fixing the what ifs. No amount of putting other people's needs ahead of your own.

The only way out of this is to replace your martyrdom response pattern with a new pattern—one that puts your oxygen mask on before anyone else's.

QUESTIONS
1. How are you being a martyr in your current circumstances?
2. Who is being a martyr benefiting? You? Your kids? Your co-parent?
3. What would you need to change to stop being a martyr?

CHALLENGE

This week we challenge you to not be a martyr. Not even once. As soon as you hear the word *should* in your head, stop everything you are doing and adjust.

"THEY SILENTLY STEPPED OUT OF THE RACE THAT THEY NEVER WANTED TO BE IN, FOUND THEIR OWN LANE, AND PROCEEDED TO WIN."
—UNKNOWN

TAKE CARE CHECKLIST
- ☐ How much sleep are you getting?
- ☐ How often do you get into nature?
- ☐ Have you taken a bath, Jacuzzi or sauna?
- ☐ Have you completed the Trigger Challenge?
- ☐ Are you spending time with friends?
- ☐ When was the last time you read a book for pleasure?
- ☐ Have you taken a walk recently?
- ☐ How often do you move your body?
- ☐ Are you eating well?
- ☐ Do you mediate? Yoga?

BOUNDARIES
PART 1

Boundaries. Blech! Have you ever met anyone who likes boundaries? There are a few but most people struggle with setting boundaries. But why? Why are boundaries so uncomfortable?

Christine Morgan, author of Happily Imperfect said it best regarding boundaries: "Setting boundaries is a way of caring for myself. It doesn't make me mean, selfish, or uncaring (just) because I don't do things your way. I care about me too.

Boundaries are uncomfortable because you've been brainwashed by a master manipulator to believe that any kind of self-care, self-preservation or self-love is not just selfish but unwarranted and only good people are worthy of taking care of themselves. You've been told for months, years, decades that you are not worthy. Add to it that you have not have had a childhood role model to teach you good boundaries.

You tell yourself that as soon as the chaos settles down, then you will go to that yoga class, or start hiking, or clean out your closets, or cook a healthy meal, or even just unplug from technology for an hour. You tell yourself that self-love and self-care work for others but their conflict isn't as crazy as yours. You tell yourself that you just need a week without drama for you to even figure out what boundaries you need to create. Who has time to figure out the boundaries they need when they are drowning?

But right now, while the chaos is at an all-time high (isn't it always at an all-time high?) you tell yourself that you just need to try to contain the conflict and if you were to try and implement a boundary, the wheels would come off the freight train and everything would fall apart to an even worse state than it is right now.

If your response pattern is to hold off on creating boundaries for fear of what your high-conflict co-parent's reaction might be, then you've created a comfort zone in your conflict.

- "But I hate the conflict, I just want peace."
- "But the boundaries will make it worse."
- "But what if I implement the wrong boundary?"

Excuses. To keep you in your comfort zone.

As horrific as your situation is, you've become skilled at convincing yourself that you are managing the conflict as best you can. Advice from friends or family on how to improve your situation is met with the thought that it won't work for you and your situation. Or you tried setting a boundary and ended up feeling like it was hard and mucky, so you quit and tell yourself the boundary didn't work.

But the truth is, you didn't give the boundary much of a chance to work. Your comfort zone is an easier place to live than in the unknown and unstable place of boundaries and self-care. You can choose to continue to operate as you have in the past—in your response pattern of not implementing boundaries—and a year from now, nothing will have changed, except that you will likely have more gray hairs and many sleepless nights.

Or you can embrace a new pattern, one that forces you to put you first before anyone else regardless of how uncomfortable it is. Because what you allow is what will continue.

What will you allow?

"ONE OF THE BEST DECISIONS YOU CAN EVER MAKE IS TO RETIRE FROM DRAMA AND DISTANCE YOURSELF FROM THE PEOPLE WHO LOVE IT."

—UNKNOWN

FEELINGS TO MOVE
☐ Fear

QUESTIONS

1. What have you been tolerating because it's easier than putting in a boundary?
2. What feelings arise when you think about implementing a boundary?
3. Is that feeling of implementing a boundary worse than how it feels to tolerate what you're tolerating?

CHALLENGE

This week we challenge you to create and implement one boundary to protect your self-care routine.

TAKE CARE CHECKLIST

☐ How much sleep are you getting?
☐ How often do you get into nature?
☐ Have you taken a bath, Jacuzzi or sauna?
☐ Have you completed the Trigger Challenge?
☐ Are you spending time with friends?
☐ When was the last time you read a book for pleasure?
☐ Have you taken a walk recently?
☐ How often do you move your body?
☐ Are you eating well?
☐ Do you mediate? Yoga?

TRUST

Trust is such an interesting word. But one thing is for sure, if you are co-parenting with someone who is high-conflict, you've lost some trust.

You don't trust your co-parent. You don't trust professionals. You don't trust the system that was designed to provide justice. You don't trust new people you meet. And you don't trust yourself. How can you? Trusting yourself is what got you into this mess in the first place.

You trusted your heart, you trusted the lies you were told, you trusted the institution of parenthood and you trusted the legal system to save you and your kids from the mental and emotional abuse pounded into you by your high-conflict co-parent.

Almost every time you were disappointed and felt betrayed. You vowed to never trust again. Until you do. But if you are continuously getting hurt by trusting the wrong people, the wrong institutions, or the wrong advice, then your response pattern is to blindly trust without taking responsibility for whom and what you trust.

- Blindly trusting is easy and carefree and spontaneous.
- Blindly trusting is child-like and peaceful.
- Blindly trusting doesn't take any effort.
- Blindly trusting gives your power away.

If you go back in time to the period of time when you fell in love with your co-parent, when they were love bombing you and even when the *digs* started happening, you'll likely remember a small nagging feeling that something wasn't quite right. But you wanted to believe the words that elicited those magical feelings. The love felt so real that you ignored the nagging feeling and chose instead to blindly trust that the nagging feeling wasn't real—the words were.

When you blindly trust someone or something, you are using your brain and not your heart to decide whether or not to trust. Trust is a feeling—not a rational or irrational thought.

FEELINGS = HEART
THOUGHTS = BRAIN

But in today's day and age people are taught to ignore their feelings because feelings are not measurable or scientific or trustworthy. We're taught to disengage from feelings and use our brain to understand and rationalize—this is true when you are communicating with someone who has high-conflict tendencies. But not in everyday life! The pendulum has swung too far, feelings have become shunned and thoughts have become powerful.

You need to have your feelings, experience your feelings, listen to your feelings. Just don't act while you're in a feeling.

FEELINGS TO MOVE
- ☐ Fear
- ☐ Anger
- ☐ Grief

Trust is a feeling—a nagging feeling that we often ignore because it's easier to blindly trust someone or something external. Why? Because then we can blame them when things go sideways rather than taking responsibility for whom and what we choose to trust.

Not trusting leaves you powerless. Start listening to your nagging inner voice that says "Hold on, something isn't right here". Stop blindly trusting external sources and allowing them to betray and disappoint you.

Learning to trust yourself is a super power and it will be your greatest source of freedom.

QUESTIONS
1. Who do you trust?
2. How can you learn to trust yourself?
3. How can you show your kids what trustworthy looks like?

CHALLENGE
This week we challenge you to close your eyes and speak kindly to yourself. Tell yourself that you are going to start trusting you again and that you need some help. 1x a day, 7 days.

"TO BE A HERO FOR ANYONE ELSE, YOU FIRST HAVE TO BE A HERO TO YOURSELF."
—NATALIE BARDO

TAKE CARE CHECKLIST
- ☐ How much sleep are you getting?
- ☐ How often do you get into nature?
- ☐ Have you taken a bath, Jacuzzi or sauna?
- ☐ Have you completed the Trigger Challenge?
- ☐ Are you spending time with friends?
- ☐ When was the last time you read a book for pleasure?
- ☐ Have you taken a walk recently?
- ☐ How often do you move your body?
- ☐ Are you eating well?
- ☐ Do you mediate? Yoga?

GUILT

Guilt is a feeling of responsibility or remorse for some offense, crime, or wrong, whether real or imagined.

Oh, the story you've created in your head about how you've destroyed your kids by giving them a parent who is so manipulative and controlling. You've read the studies and the stats and you know that children who grow up in toxic conflict are more likely to do drugs and drop out of school.

So you beat yourself up as if it's somehow all your fault that the relationship with their other parent didn't work out and that their other parent has high-conflict tendencies.

You spend thousands on legal fees trying to save your kids from the abuse you experienced, all to save them from the ongoing side effects of living in toxic conflict. When the system fails, your guilt over what you could have, should have, or would have done differently takes over.

- Guilt is a powerful feeling—one that will take you to the depths of despair every time it raises its ugly head.
- Guilt convinces you that everything wrong in your life, in your kid's lives, is your fault.
- Guilt is heavy, manipulative and often misplaced.
- Guilt keeps you stuck in the past.

It's hard not to believe the lies that are incessantly thrown our way by our co-parent about how every miniscule perceived wrong is somehow our fault. You're not smart enough. You're not organized enough. You're not disciplining enough. You're not feeding them right. You're crazy. You're making your kids crazy. You're the one who is controlling and manipulative. You wear the wrong clothes, chose the wrong dentist, got the kids the wrong haircut.

You feel guilty about being a poor parent and you feel guilty about not giving your kids the childhood you think they should have had and you feel guilty that you have allowed everything to unfold as it has.

If feeling guilt is your response pattern then you are continuing to accept blame for that which you cannot change.

Forgiving yourself is as important as forgiving others. Guilt is toxic. Guilt causes you to relive the mistake over and over. Instead, love yourself and forgive yourself.

FEELINGS TO MOVE

- ☐ Worry
- ☐ Fear

QUESTIONS

1. What do you feel guilty about?
2. How is feeling guilt benefiting you? Your kids?
3. What does the opposite of guilt feel like?

CHALLENGE

This week we challenge you to feel your guilt and let it go. Parenting through guilt is a recipe for disaster. Parent through love, and self-love. Your children will be stronger because of it.

TAKE CARE CHECKLIST

- ☐ How much sleep are you getting?
- ☐ How often do you get into nature?
- ☐ Have you taken a bath, Jacuzzi or sauna?
- ☐ Have you completed the Trigger Challenge?
- ☐ Are you spending time with friends?
- ☐ When was the last time you read a book for pleasure?
- ☐ Have you taken a walk recently?
- ☐ How often do you move your body?
- ☐ Are you eating well?
- ☐ Do you mediate? Yoga?

"SOMETIMES YOU JUST HAVE TO BE DONE. NOT MAD, NOT UPSET. JUST DONE."

—UNKNOWN

PROGRESS CHECK-IN

TAKING CARE OF ME

3 ACTIVITIES outside my norm that improved my mood

1. _____
2. _____
3. _____

IMPROVING MY CO-PARENTING

3 STEPS I took to improve my co-parenting situation

1. _____
2. _____
3. _____

PROGRESS TO MAKE

1 SITUATION in which I could have done better with my co-parent or my kids

_____

_____

MY SUCESSES

1 SITUATION I did well and I'm proud of

_____

_____

REMINDERS

☐ Didn't take my frustration out on my kids
☐ Said something positive to my kids about their other parent, new partner, or grandparents (other family)
☐ Didn't yell at my kids
☐ BIFF'D all my written messages before sending them to my co-parent
☐ Reminded myself that I've got this!
☐ Reminded myself daily that I'm the only one who can manage my own emotions and behaviors

GOALS FOR NEXT MONTH

MY JOURNAL

WEEK 21

UNSETTLED

You know that feeling that you can't name but you know it feels awful? Like you're waiting for something but you don't know what you're waiting for?

It's almost like you're waiting for the next shoe to drop, but you're out of shoes. There are no more shoes in your closet to drop. They have been dropped, chewed, or destroyed.

It feels like if anything else went wrong you'd collapse into a pile of angry, exhausted tears on the floor and you may never get up again. You are that tired, that afraid, or that unsettled.

You can't shake that feeling that doom is just around the corner. Or, if you aren't on high alert, your co-parent will sneakily find a way to slip something by you and you will _____ (fill in the blank with your worst-case scenario).

Wait, you don't know what your worst-case scenario is? If you don't know what your worst-case scenario is then your response pattern is to keep yourself unsettled so that you are permanently in fight or flight.

You say you hate that feeling of not knowing when another shoe will drop, yet you continue to keep yourself there. You might be telling yourself that the lies and manipulations are so out-of-control that you really don't know when the next shoe will drop; that you must keep your guard up because you can't possibly handle any more attacks.

What if you could move from feeling guarded and unsettled to un-clenched and grounded? Did you just roll your eyes?

Your unsettled feeling, the one that keeps you incessantly checking your email in case your co-parent has emailed. Or checking the locks ten times before you go to bed or snapping at your kids not because they were bad but because your patience is fried from living in a fight or flight state. This feeling is a response pattern you created to keep you safe because at the time you created it you didn't know that there were alternatives.

It worked! It did keep you safe! Your response pattern worked! But it's not working anymore. You think if you just increased your vigilance to protect yourself and your kids and put up higher fences around your heart so you didn't get hurt, that your feeling of being unsettled would go away.

That's the same thinking that created your unsettledness in the first place. More control, more guarding your heart, more security, more court orders. But more of anything won't settle you.

If you want to shift your response pattern from feeling unsettled to feeling settled, you have to do that from within and let go of all the false systems you have believed will keep you safe.

FEELINGS TO MOVE
- ☐ Fear
- ☐ Worry
- ☐ Over-excited.

QUESTIONS
1. What does unsettled feel like for you?
2. When was the last time you didn't feel unsettled?
3. How is feeling unsettled benefiting you?

CHALLENGE
This week we challenge you to do one activity that is outside your comfort zone. What is it? When will you do it?

TAKE CARE CHECKLIST
- ☐ How much sleep are you getting?
- ☐ How often do you get into nature?
- ☐ Have you taken a bath, Jacuzzi or sauna?
- ☐ Have you completed the Trigger Challenge?
- ☐ Are you spending time with friends?
- ☐ When was the last time you read a book for pleasure?
- ☐ Have you taken a walk recently?
- ☐ How often do you move your body?
- ☐ Are you eating well?
- ☐ Do you mediate? Yoga?

"DO YOUR CHILDREN A FAVOR AND RAISE THEM TO BE OK WITH PEOPLE NOT LIKING THEM."
—UNKNOWN

RESISTANCE

You know how to eat well, yet you often find yourself grabbing the sweets from the coffee room at work.
You know how many steps to get in a day, yet you choose Netflix over a walk.

You know at your core that what you've read in these weekly guides is true, yet you can't seem to stop yourself from engaging. You've tried self-care, self-love, self-whatever you want to call it and sure, it felt good but it wasn't sustainable.

You have a high-conflict co-parent, which means you are engaged in a full-time battle and if you aren't on all the time, you might get side swiped by your co-parent when you aren't looking. Or when you were busy doing self-care.

How could you possibly make self-care a routine when you don't have time for ongoing self-care? What if something awful happens while you're not on your phone? You would never get over the guilt while you were busy being self-indulgent.

Come on, you know you view self-care as self-indulgent. Something you can do once the conflict subsides or when you happen to find yourself with an extra hour one day. It's definitely not something you do daily. What would people think?

You have created the response pattern of *resistance* to self-care to keep you safe from internal and external judgement.

You go around fixing everyone else's problems for them, keeping busy with a to-do list a mile long that never seems to get shorter; volunteering for 18,000 jobs at your kid's school or sports teams; saying yes when you want to be saying no to events you have no interest in attending. You have binge-watched every episode of every show on Netflix. Twice.

You. Are. Busy.

But why? What is staying busy accomplishing?

It's distracting you from being present, from feeling the feels you don't want to feel. It's your resistance to self-care. If you weren't so busy, you'd have no excuses to not put a little time, energy and effort into you. Did you feel a shiver reading this? That's the resistance you are feeling towards self-care.

Internal Judgement Resistance: I don't have time, I should be doing x, y and z. I can't afford it. I need to prepare for my court case. I'm too tired. I'm not worthy. Who do you think you are? You've screwed up your kid's lives; thus, you don't deserve to take care of yourself.

External Judgement Resistance: You are repeatedly told by your co-parent that you aren't worthy, that you're a horrible parent, you waste money, and if you have so much time on your hands you should get a better job and make some real money.

FEELINGS TO MOVE
- ☐ Fear
- ☐ Worry
- ☐ Over-excited.

QUESTIONS
1. What are you resisting?
2. How is that resistance affecting your life?
3. How is the resistance benefiting you?

CHALLENGE
This week we challenge you to do 15 jumping jacks a day. All at once or broken up. But each day, do 15.

TAKE CARE CHECKLIST
- ☐ How much sleep are you getting?
- ☐ How often do you get into nature?
- ☐ Have you taken a bath, Jacuzzi or sauna?
- ☐ Have you completed the Trigger Challenge?
- ☐ Are you spending time with friends?
- ☐ When was the last time you read a book for pleasure?
- ☐ Have you taken a walk recently?
- ☐ How often do you move your body?
- ☐ Are you eating well?
- ☐ Do you mediate? Yoga?

Instead of fighting the feelings of resistance, the knowing you have that self-care is the only thing that will help you be the best version of you, you put self-care on the back burner—again.

Shifting your *resistance* response pattern towards self-care/self-love will be key in your high-conflict co-parenting success.

"YOU ARE UNHAPPY BECAUSE YOU ARE NOT IN ALIGNMENT WITH WHO YOU ARE. NOT BECAUSE OF WHAT ANYONE ELSE IS DOING."

—MARYAM HASNAA

WEEK 23

PAUSE

When was the last time you hit pause on your life? On your conflict? Does never sound about right? You've never hit a pause?

Because if you hit pause your life will fall apart? Your conflict will escalate? Your kids will suffer? You'll stop being able to put out all the fires your co-parent creates? You'll have to sit with all the awful feelings whirling around inside telling you that this situation you're in is all your fault? You might crumble and someone needs to be strong for the kids?

There are a million and five reasons you're telling yourself why you can't hit pause. Even the mere concept of it probably sparks a feeling of disgust and blasphemy.

- "I can't do that!"
- "Surely you don't understand how bad MY conflict is. If I hit pause my entire world will fall apart!"
- "If I hit pause, who would manage the kids? The drama? The lies and manipulations? The? The? The?"

You're right. If you hit pause, no one would do what you're currently doing. No one would manage everything for you. No one would defend the lies and manipulations. No one would know how bad YOUR conflict is.

How is managing all of that working for you right now? Are you any further ahead today than you were six months ago? Eighteen months ago? Five years ago? Probably not. This is because your conflict is not regular conflict. It is extraordinary conflict. It is gift that keeps on giving.

If you don't learn how to hit pause, your conflict will eventually make you sick with worry, anxiety, anger, sorrow and a litany of other emotions. You probably already feel all those feelings. How could you not? Your conflict is its own entity (I do understand! I've been there!).

The inability to hit pause on your life and conflict is a response pattern keeps you engaged in the co-parenting conflict. As you move toward having the strength to hit pause your world will slow down. Fires will burn themselves out. Sleep will happen. An inner calmness you haven't felt in years or maybe decades will take over.

Learning to hit pause is a response pattern that takes a lot of work to re-wire. Not only does your co-parent tell you everything needs to happen ASAP, but new technologies put the pressure on. You may think if you hit pause, you might miss something.

So what? You might miss something and some fires might burn longer than if you weren't putting your conflict on pause. You might not respond to an email in 24 hours. It might be 72 hours. You might not see an emergent text until 10 hours later. You might, you just might, learn that that's all okay anyway.

You don't need to be a living life/managing conflict superhero.

You are allowed to hit pause.

"HAPPY PEOPLE FOCUS ON WHAT THEY HAVE. UNHAPPY PEOPLE FOCUS ON WHAT'S MISSING."

—UNKNOWN

FEELINGS TO MOVE
- ☐ Over-excited
- ☐ Fear
- ☐ Worry
- ☐ Anger
- ☐ Grief

QUESTIONS
1. What would happen if you hit pause?
2. Now that that's out of your system, what would really happen if you hit pause?
3. What feelings come up when you imagine your life on pause?

CHALLENGE
This week we challenge you to hit pause, once, for 30 minutes. Thirty minutes without thinking about your co-parent, rushing to do your to do list, or worrying about what you're doing wrong. Just hit pause.

TAKE CARE CHECKLIST
- ☐ How much sleep are you getting?
- ☐ How often do you get into nature?
- ☐ Have you taken a bath, Jacuzzi or sauna?
- ☐ Have you completed the Trigger Challenge?
- ☐ Are you spending time with friends?
- ☐ When was the last time you read a book for pleasure?
- ☐ Have you taken a walk recently?
- ☐ How often do you move your body?
- ☐ Are you eating well?
- ☐ Do you mediate? Yoga?

THE VOICE

You know that voice in your head that agrees with everything your co-parent says? Maybe it doesn't agree with your co-parent, but it definitely leans in your co-parent's favor?

You could be in the grocery store, or trying to fall asleep and the voice in your head starts going through the words you've had yelled or emailed at you. The voice starts reliving your past, telling you all the places you couldn't have improved the situation so that your current challenges wouldn't be so horrific.

"If I had just done what she/he asked the first time without questioning it."

"If I had just responded within the hour like he/she'd asked, maybe there wouldn't be a court application."

"If I'd kept a tidier house, kept the kid's quieter or made more money at work, then maybe she/he would hate me less."

"If I'd just been more of everything I'm not, maybe this wouldn't have to be so bad."

"This is all my fault."

The voice in your head can be a dangerous one if you don't know it's there and/or you don't know how to manage it. The voice tells you you're awesome 10% of the time and reminds you of every single negative flaw you have 90% of the time.

The voice also tells you lies about yourself. If the voice in your head is telling you lies about yourself, and you aren't managing it, you are much more susceptible to the lies your co-parent is saying to you, about you, to anyone who will listen.

Suddenly, your co-parent's lies take on that much more meaning because it's not just them telling you the lies, it's also the voice in your head. Maybe your co-parent and your voice are right? Maybe this is all your fault?

If your survival pattern is to listen to the voice without wiki-checking it's validity or accuracy, then your pattern is to give away your power in an effort to keep you safe. But it's the voice in my head, you say. It has to be right. It has to be on my side. It's mine. The voice in my head should be my power.

Except it's not. At least not yet.

The voice in your head is being powered by layers and layers of trauma. Trauma from someone in your grade 4 class calling you fat and trauma from the everyday subtle, mean manipulations from someone who is supposed to love you.

Trauma has no boundaries or guidelines and it affects everyone differently. Except for the voice. Everyone who has experienced trauma without having the supports in place to process and move through it will have a voice in their head telling them lies.

The voice in your head, left unchecked, tries to keep you safe by making sure you don't rattle the status quo. Your response pattern, listening to the voice, has kept you right where the voice wants you—small and safe, in a tiny little box, full of self-loathing and fear.

FEELINGS TO MOVE

- ☐ Fear
- ☐ Worry
- ☐ Anger

Once you're aware of the voice response pattern, you can start calling the voice on its lies and manipulations. Calling the voice on its b.s.is a hard one to shift, but 100% necessary to take back your personal power and regain control of your life.

QUESTIONS

1. What does the voice in your head say when you're happy?
2. What does the voice in your head say when you're triggered?
3. What would it feel like to be able to quiet the voice?

CHALLENGE

This week we challenge you to focus on what is instead of what if.

"EVERY TIME A DECISION IS MADE, A PATH EMERGES."
— ALEXANDER DEN HEIJER

TAKE CARE CHECKLIST

- ☐ How much sleep are you getting?
- ☐ How often do you get into nature?
- ☐ Have you taken a bath, Jacuzzi or sauna?
- ☐ Have you completed the Trigger Challenge?
- ☐ Are you spending time with friends?
- ☐ When was the last time you read a book for pleasure?
- ☐ Have you taken a walk recently?
- ☐ How often do you move your body?
- ☐ Are you eating well?
- ☐ Do you mediate? Yoga?

PROGRESS CHECK-IN

TAKING CARE OF ME

3 ACTIVITIES outside my norm that improved my mood

1. _____

2. _____

3. _____

IMPROVING MY CO-PARENTING

3 STEPS I took to improve my co-parenting situation

1. _____

2. _____

3. _____

PROGRESS TO MAKE

1 SITUATION in which I could have done better with my co-parent or my kids

_____

_____

MY SUCESSES

1 SITUATION I did well and I'm proud of

_____

_____

REMINDERS

- ☐ Didn't take my frustration out on my kids
- ☐ Said something positive to my kids about their other parent, new partner, or grandparents (other family)
- ☐ Didn't yell at my kids
- ☐ BIFF'D all my written messages before sending them to my co-parent
- ☐ Reminded myself that I've got this!
- ☐ Reminded myself daily that I'm the only one who can manage my own emotions and behaviors

GOALS FOR NEXT MONTH

MY JOURNAL

NICE

If you've asked yourself on occasion how you landed in a high-conflict situation, you're not alone.

The common thread through all of the high-conflict co-parents I've worked with is this—like you, they're all nice people

- You don't give up on tough situations—you actively work to resolve them instead, because you're nice.
- You don't let people suffer in silence—you reach out and offer support, because you're nice.
- You don't walk away from people who need you—you roll up your sleeves and help them, because your nice.

How is being nice a bad thing? Aren't we taught to be nice from birth?

Being nice is giving your time and energy to someone in hopes that they will appreciate the gesture. Being nice is giving in hopes of getting. And it's not usually on purpose.

You aren't being nice to be manipulative. In fact, nothing could be further from the truth.

You are being nice because deep down, in areas of you that might not have been explored yet, you are being nice in hopes that the person you are being nice to will be nice back to you. Because if they're nice back to you, that gives you validation that you are a nice person.

If your response pattern is to be nice to people, all people, without first fact-checking their stories, then your response pattern is to hope that if you're nice to them, they'll be nice back.

Because if they're nice back, that reinforces your ego that you are in fact a nice person.

Have you heard the quip that nice people finish last? In many cases it is true. Nice people finish last because on their hierarchy of people they put first, nice people put themselves last. Nice people lack the boundaries needed to discern whether or not they have the time, energy or ability to help—they just jump in and help, hoping the person they help will think they are nice.

"Being nice knows no boundaries." – A.L.

Instead of being nice, choose kindness. Even the language used in the last sentence illustrates the difference between being nice and choosing kindness.

Being nice.

Choosing kindness.

Choosing kindness allows you to pick and choose who you help, when you help, and why you help. Choosing kindness gives pause to the impulsivity of being nice, allowing you to decide if your time and energy are a match for what/who needs help and support.

Shifting your response pattern from being nice (putting others needs ahead of your own) to choosing kindness (purposefully deciding where to put your time and energy) will help you realign your sense of self-worth.

"THE PAUSE BEFORE WE ACT IS THE SPACE WHERE WE RECLAIM OUR POWER."

—YUNG PUEBLO

FEELINGS TO MOVE

- ☐ Fear
- ☐ Anger
- ☐ Grief
- ☐ Over-Excited
- ☐ Worry

QUESTIONS

1. What does the difference between nice and kind mean to you?
2. How can you manage yourself so that you behave kindly moving forward? And not just 'nice'?
3. How has being nice benefited you so far?

CHALLENGE

This week we challenge you to write 500 words on how you can show up as 'kind' in your life, rather than 'nice.'

TAKE CARE CHECKLIST

- ☐ How much sleep are you getting?
- ☐ How often do you get into nature?
- ☐ Have you taken a bath, Jacuzzi or sauna?
- ☐ Have you completed the Trigger Challenge?
- ☐ Are you spending time with friends?
- ☐ When was the last time you read a book for pleasure?
- ☐ Have you taken a walk recently?
- ☐ How often do you move your body?
- ☐ Are you eating well?
- ☐ Do you mediate? Yoga?

WEEK 26

HOPE

Hope is an interesting word. To have hope means you are optimistic the future won't be as bleak as the present. To not have hope means you've lost all optimism that the future will be any different than it is right now.

Optimists don't just take the crappy hand they were dealt and cope with it—they actively seek out options and possibilities to change the game.

Without hope, you become a victim of circumstance. You become someone who chooses to live with the crappy hand they were dealt, rather than explore options to re-deal the cards.

Without a doubt, if you are co-parenting with a high-conflict person, your current circumstances are the worst of the worst. You are co-parenting with a manipulative, controlling, threatening, and intimidating human being. You are constantly on guard, waiting for the next shoe to drop. Your character and your ability to parent are attacked on a regular basis. You can't say or do anything right because everything is twisted and manipulated into a negative.

You're feeling like you've run out of hope, that you've done everything in your power to try and make your horrific situation better. Your once optimistic self has turned into a shell of itself and you feel like giving up.

You are co-parenting with someone who is hell-bent on destroying you, who twists everything you say into a negative, and who manipulates words and situations to make you look bad. Yet you keep trying to find ways to improve the co-parenting relationship.

Your mind is always looking for possibilities to make the co-parenting relationship better.

Your response pattern is to have hope, to be optimistic, despite yourself. Your response pattern keeps you searching for the one thing you haven't tried yet to try and make your situation survivable.

You think things like:

- "What if I tried only communicating by email, maybe then he/she would choose words more carefully?"
- "What if I only enrolled the kids in activities during the times that I have them, that way we don't need to agree on which activities to put the kids into?"
- "What if I made all the exchanges happen at school or daycare, then we wouldn't need to see each other?"
- "What if I just gave him/her everything they want, maybe then the attacks would end?"

OR

What if you accepted that your co-parent is never going to change and that the only way out of this mess is to stop having hope that the situation will change and start putting that energy into yourself.

FEELINGS TO MOVE
- ☐ Grief

QUESTIONS
1. How has the hope/disappointment cycle showed up in your life?
2. What feeling pattern has the hope/disappointment cycle created in you?
3. How has hoping your co-parent will change benefited you?

CHALLENGE
This week we challenge you to notice when you feel hope around your co-parent potentially changing and ask yourself why?

TAKE CARE CHECKLIST
- ☐ How much sleep are you getting?
- ☐ How often do you get into nature?
- ☐ Have you taken a bath, Jacuzzi or sauna?
- ☐ Have you completed the Trigger Challenge?
- ☐ Are you spending time with friends?
- ☐ When was the last time you read a book for pleasure?
- ☐ Have you taken a walk recently?
- ☐ How often do you move your body?
- ☐ Are you eating well?
- ☐ Do you mediate? Yoga?

If your response pattern is to have hope that your co-parent might see the light and shift their behavior, then you are in for a long and torturous existence. Shift that response pattern of hoping for a different future into loving yourself in the present moment and that will spark the transformation in you have been hoping for.

"YOUR DAY IS PRETTY MUCH FORMED BY HOW YOU SPEND YOUR FIRST HOUR. CHECK YOUR THOUGHTS, ATTITUDE AND HEART."

—UNKNOWN

FAIR

It's not fair that I only see the kids 50% of the time; It's not fair that the kids can't see me on my birthday; It's not fair that he/she gave up on the marriage/relationship and I'm the one suffering; It's not fair that I can't see or speak with my kids every day…

…It's not fair that he/she was an absent parent while we were together and now she/he is the super parent; It's not fair that I have to pay child support."

WHAT DOES FAIR REALLY MEAN?

Looking through many dictionaries, they seem to agree that fairness means what is right or acceptable and not favoring one person over another.

Well, that sounds reasonable.

The definition of fair when it comes to divorce and co-parenting means to have a reasonably kind and mutually respectful relationship with your child's other parent for the sake of your children. Yet so many parents in high-conflict situations report that their experience with their high-conflict co-parent is anything but fair.

LIKE BEAUTY, FAIR IS IN THE EYES OF THE BEHOLDER.

If you wanted something in your divorce or separation and got it, chances are you would view the outcome as fair. If you wanted something in your divorce or separation and didn't get it, you'd view the outcome as unfair.

What parents often forget is that divorce or separation isn't fair. Rarely is the decision to end a relationship mutual. Rarely do both parents feel only one parent should have all the decision-making authority and time with the children. Rarely (never) do either end up financially advantaged.

What the dictionary definitions leave out is that fairness is a perception created by parents to meet their own needs and wants. If your response pattern is to continuously say to yourself (or anyone who will listen) that the situation just isn't fair, then you are allowing yourself to succumb to the poor me syndrome. The poor me syndrome gives your power to an external source. Your goal in thriving instead of barely surviving when you are co-parenting with an HCP is to regain your power.

You are in a co-parenting relationship with someone who seems to hates you, and seems to want to destroy you, regardless of who might get hurt in the process.

NOTHING ABOUT YOUR SITUATION IS FAIR.

But dwelling on what isn't fair continues to put energy into what you can't change. The courts aren't going to magically change one day. Your co-parent isn't likely to either.

So instead of dwelling on what isn't fair—a response pattern that gives away your power—focus instead on what is going right in your life, like your family, your job, or other friendships. It might be something as small as reminding yourself that you all woke up healthy today or that you have to play Monopoly tonight or the sun shined today.

Shifting the it's not fair response pattern to one of small appreciations will be one of the biggest changes you can make for a better, brighter future regardless of what your co-parent might sling at you.

> "YOU OWE YOURSELF
> ONE HOUR A DAY OF
> SELF-MAINTENANCE.
> IT CAN INCLUDE READING,
> WRITING, YOGA, EXERCISE,
> DANCING, MEDITATION,
> PAINTING, OR WHATEVER,
> BUT YOU OWE IT
> TO YOURSELF.
> ONE HOUR, 1/24,
> OF YOUR DAY.
> THAT'S LESS THAN 5%.
> IT MATTERS.
> IT REALLY DOES.
> MAKE IT COUNT."
>
> —JIM CAREY

FEELINGS TO MOVE
- ☐ Grief
- ☐ Fear
- ☐ Anger

QUESTIONS
1. How do you define fair?
2. Knowing that this situation will never be fair, what are your options for moving forward?
3. How has being attached to what is fair benefited you?

CHALLENGE
This week we challenge you to go on 3 walks in nature. 10-minute walks, 30-minute walks, 3-hour walks. The length doesn't matter. Just get outside and walk. Three times.

TAKE CARE CHECKLIST
- ☐ How much sleep are you getting?
- ☐ How often do you get into nature?
- ☐ Have you taken a bath, Jacuzzi or sauna?
- ☐ Have you completed the Trigger Challenge?
- ☐ Are you spending time with friends?
- ☐ When was the last time you read a book for pleasure?
- ☐ Have you taken a walk recently?
- ☐ How often do you move your body?
- ☐ Are you eating well?
- ☐ Do you mediate? Yoga?

DESPAIR

Despair is best described as that feeling of wanting to run away from your life and start over, but knowing you can't because you are trapped by a court order that says you can't travel with your kids without permission.

For a brief moment you imagine what it would be like to change all your identities run away anonymously. It's a brief moment, maybe 5-7 seconds (because you know it's a fantasy and that it's entirely against the law and against your children's best interests), but in that brief moment you experience lightness—a millisecond of possibility. Then your email alerts you to a new message and your brief dance with freedom is squashed like a bug on pavement.

Your real life is the opposite of lightness and possibility.

You are controlled, manipulated, verbally and emotionally abused, exhausted and desperate for someone, anyone, to save you. You are strong and independent, brave and courageous and yet you just want to be saved. Even a wizard with a wand will do. Please, someone save me!

If your response pattern is to go into despair, feeling like life as you know it is hopeless and nothing will be better until you are saved from this situation, then you are stuck in a pattern of wanting an external source to fix an internal problem. No person or system can save you from the hell you are experiencing right now except yourself. That sounds cliché but it's much deeper than a cliché.

Your high-conflict co-parent will suck your soul and feed it to the wildebeests if you let him/her because they are relentless in their pursuit of ruining you. Falling into despair fuels their ruthless attempts to hurt and minimize you.

TRY THIS: get down and dirty with allowing yourself to feel extreme sadness over the life you could have lived if you had just had kids with someone else. And I mean cry tears that make your stomach muscles hurt. Cry until your shoulders stop hanging out at your ears. Cry until you fall asleep.

Just make sure you are crying with purpose, crying to move your feelings of despair. Crying for the sake of crying allows the story of despair to continue in your head.

But crying with purpose and intention, allows you to feel those horrible feelings more deeply and thus allowing you to move through them rather than become them. Crying with intention clears out old, stagnant energy to make room for new, clearer thoughts and possibilities.

Your despair response pattern has kept you safe long enough. It's time to move through despair and feel real life possibility, not just imagined freedom.

"BEING REALISTIC IS THE MOST COMMONLY TRAVELLED ROAD TO MEDIOCRITY."

—WILL SMITH

FEELINGS TO MOVE
- ☐ Grief

QUESTIONS
1. When was the last time you cried? Not circumstantial crying, but surrendering to what is crying?
2. What does despair feel like inside you?
3. What would happen if you let yourself feel it? Fully?

CHALLENGE
This week we challenge you to write 500 words on despair.

TAKE CARE CHECKLIST
- ☐ How much sleep are you getting?
- ☐ How often do you get into nature?
- ☐ Have you taken a bath, Jacuzzi or sauna?
- ☐ Have you completed the Trigger Challenge?
- ☐ Are you spending time with friends?
- ☐ When was the last time you read a book for pleasure?
- ☐ Have you taken a walk recently?
- ☐ How often do you move your body?
- ☐ Are you eating well?
- ☐ Do you mediate? Yoga?

PROGRESS CHECK-IN

TAKING CARE OF ME

3 ACTIVITIES outside my norm that improved my mood

1. _____

2. _____

3. _____

IMPROVING MY CO-PARENTING

3 STEPS I took to improve my co-parenting situation

1. _____

2. _____

3. _____

PROGRESS TO MAKE

1 SITUATION in which I could have done better with my co-parent or my kids

_____

_____

MY SUCESSES

1 SITUATION I did well and I'm proud of

_____

_____

REMINDERS

- ☐ Didn't take my frustration out on my kids
- ☐ Said something positive to my kids about their other parent, new partner, or grandparents (other family)
- ☐ Didn't yell at my kids
- ☐ BIFF'D all my written messages before sending them to my co-parent
- ☐ Reminded myself that I've got this!
- ☐ Reminded myself daily that I'm the only one who can manage my own emotions and behaviors

GOALS FOR NEXT MONTH

MY JOURNAL

PROCRASTINATION

Have you put your life on hold until your co-parenting relationship gets better? Do you find yourself planning for the day your kids are 18 and you no longer have to communicate as much with their other parent? Are you too tired to eat well, go to the gym, or have a shower? Has Netflix become your best friend?

If your response pattern is to procrastinate until life gets a little easier, then it's time to move through your perceived comfort zone and dive head first into living.

Sure, your life may have its own special flavor of hard (co-parenting with someone who is high-conflict, next to losing a child to death, will likely be the hardest experience of your life) but that doesn't mean you put your life on hold and wait until it's calmer to have fun, to fall in love, to laugh.

Procrastinating life because you're too tired, your life is too complicated, or because you are paralyzed in fear of what might happen next is your comfort zone talking. Your comfort zone wants you to:

- Wait until your world calms down before you embark any adventures
- Figure out your whole life before you invite someone to share it with you
- Wait until your co-parent is nicer before you let yourself enjoy time with friends
- Wait to have a belly laugh

Your comfort zone tells you that you aren't worthy of laughter and joy, freedom and experience, not until you learn to better manage your co-parenting relationship.

But here's the thing—your co-parenting relationship isn't going to get any better if you are procrastinating living life waiting for it to get better. Your co-parenting relationship will only get better once you stop procrastinating, leap out of your comfort zone (hold your breath if you have to) and start living life on your terms, not your co-parent's or anyone else's.

Regardless of what you do or say, how you choose to live or not live your life, it won't be good enough for your co-parent. They will always find a way to minimize your life and your being. Your procrastinating isn't going to change that. Living in your comfort zone isn't going to change that.

Challenge your procrastination response pattern, move out of your comfort zone, and explore the you that you have long ago forgotten about. Better yet, create a whole new you—a you who doesn't procrastinate life.

> "THE DEEPEST SECRET IS THAT LIFE IS NOT A PROCESS OF DISCOVERY, BUT A PROCESS OF CREATION. YOU ARE NOT DISCOVERING YOURSELF, BUT CREATING YOURSELF ANEW. SEEK THEREFORE, NOT TO FIND OUT WHO YOU ARE, BUT SEEK TO DETERMINE WHO YOU WANT TO BE."
> —UNKNOWN

FEELINGS TO MOVE
- ☐ Fear
- ☐ Grief

QUESTIONS
1. What are you procrastinating doing? Feeling?
2. What would you be doing if you weren't in a co-parenting nightmare?
3. How has procrastinating benefited you?

CHALLENGE
This week we challenge you to do the 5-second rule by Mel Robbins (see her book *The 5 Second Rule* if you like). Each time you have something to do but your inner voice wants to procrastinate, within 5 seconds start whatever it is you were procrastinating.

TAKE CARE CHECKLIST
- ☐ How much sleep are you getting?
- ☐ How often do you get into nature?
- ☐ Have you taken a bath, Jacuzzi or sauna?
- ☐ Have you completed the Trigger Challenge?
- ☐ Are you spending time with friends?
- ☐ When was the last time you read a book for pleasure?
- ☐ Have you taken a walk recently?
- ☐ How often do you move your body?
- ☐ Are you eating well?
- ☐ Do you mediate? Yoga?

CRUMBS

When did it become Ok to accept crumbs from others?
Crumbs are the leftovers that no one wants.
Crumbs are the debris of time. Crumbs are space fillers.
Crumbs hold very little value.

The crumbs you settle for define your self-worth. If you are accepting crumbs from others then it's time to put a magnifying glass to your self-worth and examine why you think that's okay—let's be clear—it's not okay.

Regardless of your job, your finances, your parenting style, your friendship circle, your romantic relationships, your hopes and dreams—you deserve more than crumbs.

If your response pattern has been to accept crumbs from others, to get excited by the crumbs your given rather than upgrade your expectations to the full piece of toast, then your feelings of not good enough are keeping you stuck and feeling hopeless. It's hard to feel awesome, regardless of the drama in your life, if you don't expect awesome from yourself and those around you.

You will never be good enough in your co-parent's eyes, never ever! And yet you have put all of your personal time, energy, and power into trying to convince them that you are good enough.

You take their crumbs when you can get them and you convince yourself that maybe this time will be different and he/she will stop criticizing me and we can be amicable. The usual outcome is to hang your head like a fool when the crumbs disappear and you are left feeling deflated, embarrassed, and angry.

Accepting crumbs reaffirms your low self-worth. Accepting crumbs has also kept you safe from feeling confident, alive, vibrant, and full of possibility. The last time you felt such optimism you ended up in a relationship with someone who has spent years or maybe even decades trying to cripple your self-esteem. Why would you want to put yourself out there again like that?

No thanks. It's so much easier to just accept crumbs and continue to feel unworthy.

Spend some time playing with why you allow your response pattern of accepting crumbs to continue and how accepting crumbs affect the stories you are telling yourself about your self-worth. For giggles, let's explore what upgrading from crumbs to toast would look like:

How not to accept crumbs with confidence?

- Believe in patterns, not apologies
- Don't fall in love with potential
- Believe red flags
- Know your worth
- Don't lower your standards

YOU ARE WORTH THE WHOLE PIECE OF TOAST!

FEELINGS TO MOVE
- ☐ Fear
- ☐ Grief
- ☐ Anger

QUESTIONS
1. Who have you been accepting crumbs from?
2. How has accepting crumbs benefited you?
3. What would it look like to not accept crumbs?

CHALLENGE
This week we challenge you to accept only toast from friends, colleagues, and loved ones. You teach people how to treat you.

TAKE CARE CHECKLIST
- ☐ How much sleep are you getting?
- ☐ How often do you get into nature?
- ☐ Have you taken a bath, Jacuzzi or sauna?
- ☐ Have you completed the Trigger Challenge?
- ☐ Are you spending time with friends?
- ☐ When was the last time you read a book for pleasure?
- ☐ Have you taken a walk recently?
- ☐ How often do you move your body?
- ☐ Are you eating well?
- ☐ Do you mediate? Yoga?

"MORE PEOPLE WOULD LEARN FROM THEIR MISTAKES IF THEY WEREN'T SO BUSY DENYING THEM."

—UNKNOWN

BALANCE

Have you given your whole life to the mysterious feeling of balance? Are you waiting until your co-parent chills out and you can get some balance in your life before you tackle anything else? Cleaning? Cooking? Your career? Dating?

Do you daydream about what balance looks like? Feels like?

Are you on a beach somewhere, totally unplugged, not the slightest bit anxious about whether or not some angry text has arrived to your turned off phone?

Are you skiing in the mountains, out of cell coverage, mentally at one with nature without a single thought about whether or not your co-parent is making a court application for primary custody?

Are you in Africa, soaking in the beauty of untouched land and the silence that such beauty affords?

Or does balance mean going one day without a cruel email from your co-parent? One week without an accusation of alienation and abuse? One month without an anxiety attack? The mysterious idea of balance is written about, spoken about, acted out on television and movies. But what is it, actually?

My definition of balance is the go-to state of mental, emotional and physical awareness that allows a feeling to pop into my being, to stay 5 minutes, and to then move along. I know, yaddda, yadda, yadda. You may think that you will never achieve balance until your co-parent moves to Mars.

Andrea Cole notes in her work that balance is "…an internal feeing, not an external destination". If balance is internal, not external, that means we can create it whenever we want.

- "But I can't create balance in my mental, emotional and physical state when my co-parent is slinging mud at me every five minutes."
- "But my internal state is a disaster, permanently stuck in fight or flight. It will take me forever to figure out how to get my internal state balanced."
- "But if I could just go away for a week so I could sort out my thoughts and feelings, then maybe I could get to that internal balance."

But. But. But. There is no but in balance.

If you genuinely want balance in your life, stop making excuses for why you can't have it and start creating it. You do it by having the awareness that balance is internal, not external, which then allows you to start putting your attention towards your internal world.

"WHAT YOU PUT YOUR ATTENTION TO GROWS STRONGER."

– MAHARISHI MAHESH

THE INTERNAL BALANCE EXERCISE

Each time you feel imbalanced, close your eyes and remind yourself that feeling imbalanced is just a feeling—a response feeling you've created to allow yourself to stay comfortable in fight or flight. I know fight or flight isn't actually comfortable but it's become a feeling you are so familiar with that the familiarity of the fight or flight feeling is what has become your comfort zone.

When the feeling of imbalance hits you, close your eyes and say, "I am choosing internal balance." Say it three times. Inhale as you mentally say to yourself, "I am choosing internal balance." Exhale quietly, without any mental chatter. Repeat. 3x.

Each month that you do this, increase how many times you repeat the sentence by three.

Month 1: 3x
Month 2: 6x
Month 3: 9x

Gone are the days of letting external circumstances control your internal feelings of balance.

"WORRY ABOUT YOUR CHARACTER, NOT YOUR REPUTATION. BECAUSE YOUR CHARACTER IS WHO YOU ARE, AND YOUR REPUTATION IS ONLY WHAT OTHERS THINK OF YOU."

—JIM CAREY

FEELINGS TO MOVE

☐ All of them

QUESTIONS

1. What does balance mean to you?
2. What will your life look like when you have balance?
3. How has not having balance benefited you?

CHALLENGE

This week (and for the next 3 months) we challenge you to do the internal balance exercise.

TAKE CARE CHECKLIST

☐ How much sleep are you getting?
☐ How often do you get into nature?
☐ Have you taken a bath, Jacuzzi or sauna?
☐ Have you completed the Trigger Challenge?
☐ Are you spending time with friends?
☐ When was the last time you read a book for pleasure?
☐ Have you taken a walk recently?
☐ How often do you move your body?
☐ Are you eating well?
☐ Do you mediate? Yoga?

LEARNED HELPLESSNESS

When you hear the phrase *learned helplessness,* you may immediately think of someone who is weak or even pathetic. Someone who has given up, given in, or worse—they've become invisible.

Someone who can't make decisions, falls into poor me patterns, and often resembles Eeyore from Winnie the Pooh.

When we see someone we perceive to be helpless, we often judge them and wonder why they can't just get their act together and leave the abusive relationship or cease the emotional engagement with their tormentor. That is, until we become one of those people.

Suddenly the box we live in becomes even smaller and it feels like we're living in a paper bag. We can't breathe. Like any wrong move will end up with an expensive court case or our children will be removed from our care. We become paralyzed in fear, terror... repeatedly.

But what if I told you that learned helplessness has an actual psychiatric definition?

The American Psychiatric Association defines it as "A phenomenon in which repeated exposure to uncontrollable stressors results in individuals failing to use any control options that may later become available. Essentially, individuals are said to learn that they lack behavioral control over environmental events, which, in turn, undermines the motivation to make changes or attempt to alter situations."

Now the phrase learned helplessness doesn't sound so wet noodle'ish anymore, does it?

To make a complicated story somewhat less complicated, let's break it down. Animals have a nerve that allows their bodies to shut down during times of stress so they don't learn helplessness. Humans don't have that same function. Our nervous system just keeps taking stressful, traumatic punches until one day you find yourself incapable of making a decision or brainstorming options to improve your situation.

It's a gradual slippery slope of trauma layered upon trauma. While humans may not have the same nerve that animals have to protect them from extended periods of stress, maybe in a round-about way learned helplessness is our nervous systems' way of shutting down to protect us from anymore trauma.

If learned helplessness is a response pattern you find yourself in, a pattern of shutting down to keep yourself safe, then awareness of the pattern is the first step to shifting the pattern. You've been through sheer hell trying to navigate the dark, murky, traumatizing waters of co-parenting with someone high-conflict.

BE. NICER. TO. YOURSELF.

Think of learned helplessness as a turtle shell that you've unintentionally created to keep you safe. Learned helplessness took your body years, maybe even decades to create. The unravelling of learned helplessness won't take as long because you are unravelling consciously. It will take time and it won't always be easy. But the other side of learned helplessness is confidence, clarity and trust.

"A SAINT WAS ASKED, 'WHAT IS ANGER?' HE GAVE A BEAUTIFUL ANSWER: 'IT IS A PUNISHMENT WE GIVE TO OURSELVES FOR SOMEBODY ELSE'S MISTAKE.'"

—UNKNOWN

FEELINGS TO MOVE

☐ Fear
☐ Anger
☐ Surrender

QUESTIONS

1. In what areas of your life have you developed a learned helplessness?
2. How does learned helplessness present itself?
3. How have you benefited from learned helplessness?

CHALLENGE

This week we challenge you to write 500 words on where your learned helplessness has stemmed from. Understanding the roots will allow you to release their hold over you.

TAKE CARE CHECKLIST

☐ How much sleep are you getting?
☐ How often do you get into nature?
☐ Have you taken a bath, Jacuzzi or sauna?
☐ Have you completed the Trigger Challenge?
☐ Are you spending time with friends?
☐ When was the last time you read a book for pleasure?
☐ Have you taken a walk recently?
☐ How often do you move your body?
☐ Are you eating well?
☐ Do you mediate? Yoga?

PROGRESS CHECK-IN

TAKING CARE OF ME

3 ACTIVITIES outside my norm that improved my mood

1. ....
2. ....
3. ....

IMPROVING MY CO-PARENTING

3 STEPS I took to improve my co-parenting situation

1. ....
2. ....
3. ....

PROGRESS TO MAKE

1 SITUATION in which I could have done better with my co-parent or my kids

....

....

MY SUCESSES

1 SITUATION I did well and I'm proud of

....

....

REMINDERS

☐ Didn't take my frustration out on my kids

☐ Said something positive to my kids about their other parent, new partner, or grandparents (other family)

☐ Didn't yell at my kids

☐ BIFF'D all my written messages before sending them to my co-parent

☐ Reminded myself that I've got this!

☐ Reminded myself daily that I'm the only one who can manage my own emotions and behaviors

GOALS FOR NEXT MONTH

MY JOURNAL

DIGESTION

How in the world are we connecting digestion to co-parenting with someone high-conflict tendencies? Actually, both figuratively AND literally!

HOW IS YOUR DIGESTION?

Does your stomach gurgle you to sleep every night (a sign of good digestion)? Or are you bloated? Uncomfortable in your jeans? Does food go in but very little comes out? Do you suffer from acid reflux? Do you love or loathe your belly? Do you struggle to gain weight? Lose weight?

If you're curious about how one of the many ways the stress of your ability (or inability) to manage your co-parenting relationship manifests in your body, then take a close look at your digestion. The quality of your digestion is a direct link to the level of stress your body is under emotionally, mentally, and physically. Manage your stress more effectively and your digestion improves.

Which means your pants will fit better, you'll sleep more soundly, and your belly will shrink.

What about diet and exercise, you say? I'm not suggesting they don't play a part in your digestion for they obviously do. I'm just saying they aren't the only game changers on your digestion.

The stress hormone cortisol is a fabulous hormone designed to keep us safe during times of attack. Cortisol is our fight or flight hormone. The one that tells us to run so we don't get eaten by a bear.

What is scarier than getting hourly, daily, weekly, monthly emails from your co-parent attacking your character and your parenting skills? Making threats to call the police, or actually calling the department of children's services to take your kids away from you?

Your body has learned to keep itself safe from the attacks by pumping out cortisol every time you hear your co-parent's name or get notified a new email or text has arrived. It's as if your body has created a negative Pavlovian response to your co-parent's existence.

Often times people don't even realize their digestion has deteriorated until it's gone, completely. And then they are left trying different food and exercise combinations to try and rebuild their digestive system. Paleo, food combining, GAPS diet. Running, spinning, rowing. When that doesn't work they start seeking out medical testing and naturopathic care. They know something is wrong, they just don't know what it is.

SOME SCIENTISTS SAY THAT THE BODY HAS TWO BRAINS, THE HEAD BRAIN AND THE STOMACH BRAIN.

If your stomach brain isn't working as well it once did, it's time to take a look at how the stress you are under is factoring in to your digestion. If this sounds like you, then your response pattern has been to jump unknowingly into fight or flight during times of stress, forcing your body to pump out excessive amounts of cortisol which results in poorer functioning of your stomach brain, which directly affects your digestion.

- How do you improve your digestion? Reduce your cortisol production.
- How do you reduce your cortisol production? Learn to manage your stress more effectively.
- How do you manage your stress more effectively? Start with self-love.

"YOU HAVE TO LEARN TO SAY NO WITHOUT FEELING GUILTY. SETTING BOUNDARIES IS HEALTHY. YOU NEED TO LEARN TO RESPECT AND TAKE CARE OF YOURSELF."

—UNKNOWN

FEELINGS TO MOVE

- ☐ Anger
- ☐ Fear
- ☐ Surrender
- ☐ Excessive giddiness
- ☐ Worry

QUESTIONS

1. How is your digestion?
2. What can you do to improve digestion?
3. When did your digestion go sideways?

CHALLENGE

This week we challenge you to eat veggies, and only veggies, for one 24-hour day. Cooked, raw, grilled, roasted—it doesn't matter.

TAKE CARE CHECKLIST

- ☐ How much sleep are you getting?
- ☐ How often do you get into nature?
- ☐ Have you taken a bath, Jacuzzi or sauna?
- ☐ Have you completed the Trigger Challenge?
- ☐ Are you spending time with friends?
- ☐ When was the last time you read a book for pleasure?
- ☐ Have you taken a walk recently?
- ☐ How often do you move your body?
- ☐ Are you eating well?
- ☐ Do you mediate? Yoga?

PLEASER

You're not alone if you keep wondering how you got into this high-conflict situation. You are an intelligent, likeable human being. How did you end up in a co-parenting relationship with someone who is so high-conflict?

What made you think having kids with them was a good idea? Sigh... just when you think you've moved on, that old nagging question pops into your head again.

SO HOW DID YOU GET INTO THIS MESS?

From a very young age you learned that when you please someone, they smile. When you don't please someone, they are indifferent towards you. Voilà! The need to please was created.

Often, pleasers go through life trying to please others and often don't even know that is what they are trying to do. Pleasing someone creates an adrenaline high and validation that we are good enough. Along the way, pleasing someone became the only way you received validation that you were good enough.

As a result, you sought out people to please—parents, teachers, friends, colleagues, employers and romantic partners. When you first met your co-parent, you were attracted to their energy (and you likely had a spark with them) and intriguing ability to sing your praises really loudly when you pleased him/her, which only fueled your need to please them further.

That high from pleasing them was addictive. So you kept trying and your internal dialogue went something like this:

- Wow, this super cool and important person thinks I'm awesome.
- Wow, with him/her in my life, I am good enough.

Then it moved to:

- Wow, I better not screw this up.
- Wow, it's getting harder and harder to please him/her.

Then finally:

- But wow, I need to make this parenting relationship better for my kids.
- But wow, if I could just find a way to please/him her and then it will all be okay.

If your response pattern is to please, then the co-parenting relationship you are navigating is going to continue to be a challenging one until you release the need to have him/her like you.

Your co-parent will never like you. It's your job to be okay with that. Not only okay with not being liked, but indifferent towards it. Indifference isn't a lack of caring.

Indifference is a freeing place of emotional disengagement that allows you to thrive in your life regardless of the attacks, manipulations and judgements hurled in your direction.

"WE ALL HAVE TWO LIVES. THE SECOND ONE STARTS WHEN WE REALIZE WE ONLY HAVE ONE."

—UNKNOWN

FEELINGS TO MOVE
- ☐ Fear
- ☐ Worry
- ☐ Anger

QUESTIONS
1. Reflect on your life, when did you learn to become a pleaser?
2. At what expense has pleasing others had on you?
3. How has being a pleaser benefited you?

CHALLENGE
This week we challenge you to come up with 10 things that please YOU, and put at least 2 of them into action.

TAKE CARE CHECKLIST
- ☐ How much sleep are you getting?
- ☐ How often do you get into nature?
- ☐ Have you taken a bath, Jacuzzi or sauna?
- ☐ Have you completed the Trigger Challenge?
- ☐ Are you spending time with friends?
- ☐ When was the last time you read a book for pleasure?
- ☐ Have you taken a walk recently?
- ☐ How often do you move your body?
- ☐ Are you eating well?
- ☐ Do you mediate? Yoga?

TRIGGERED

It happens to the best of us. After days, maybe even weeks, you start to feel confidence in your disengagement skills toward your co-parent. It's working!

You're sleeping at night (or at least some nights), and you're obsessing less about how to fix the conflict and focusing that energy on starting to laugh and relax a little. You think you've nailed it. You've succeeded in not letting your co-parent trigger you.

AND THEN... WHAM!

Your co-parent blindsides you with something you thought you should be prepared to handle. You rage with anger. Or cry in frustration. Freeze in fear. Your blood turns to ice. You can't breathe. Your brain shuts off. Your resolve to disengage doesn't just crumble; it shatters into a million pieces.

"I can't do this anymore."

"I want to just give up."

"I'm calling my lawyer and we're going to court."

You've been triggered. When it happens, you think all these new feelings (that are actually old feelings) are here to stay. Forever. You forget that you have skills from past experience and maybe a few you learned in this book. Skills that taught you how to move through different emotions so that you don't get stuck in them. No one is sane while stuck in emotions.

When you're triggered, the feelings you feel are intense, all-consuming, and terrifying. When you're triggered, you fall back into old, unhealthy response patterns. Your response pattern of getting triggered used to help keep you safe, but now your response pattern triggers are just keeping you stuck.

Why do you keep getting triggered? Why, when you've done so much work to get de-triggered? You get triggered when you got too busy. Too busy to practice all the self-care routines you put into place earlier in this workbook.

When you get busy, you get lazy. And when you get busy (and lazy), you don't practice all the strategies you have implemented to manage your triggers. All those skills that allow you to sleep better, relax more, enjoy life again.

Don't expect to never get triggered again, expecting such will just lead to further disappointment and frustration. Instead, move towards having an internal knowing that when you're triggered (because you will be triggered), you'll be able to move through the trigger quickly and efficiently. You won't get stuck in the feeling of being triggered for too long.

"GO 24 HOURS WITHOUT COMPLAINING. (NOT EVEN ONCE.) THEN WATCH HOW YOUR LIFE STARTS CHANGING!"

—UNKNOWN

FEELINGS TO MOVE
☐ All of them

QUESTIONS
1. What are your triggers?
2. Where do you triggers stem from?
3. How have your triggers benefited you?

CHALLENGE
This week we challenge you to pick a song, any song, and blast it as loud as you can each time you're triggered.

TAKE CARE CHECKLIST
☐ How much sleep are you getting?
☐ How often do you get into nature?
☐ Have you taken a bath, Jacuzzi or sauna?
☐ Have you completed the Trigger Challenge?
☐ Are you spending time with friends?
☐ When was the last time you read a book for pleasure?
☐ Have you taken a walk recently?
☐ How often do you move your body?
☐ Are you eating well?
☐ Do you mediate? Yoga?

BOUNDARIES
PART 2

Interestingly, very few people can actually tell you **what they do want**. Even when pushed, people will tell you what they don't want, and when you focus all your energy and attention toward what you don't want, you end up attracting just that—everything you don't want.

When you ask someone what he or she wants or needs in their co-parenting relationship, they usually begin by telling you what they don't want:

- "I don't want my ex to speak poorly of me in front of our kids."
- "I don't want the kids dropped off fifteen minutes late at every exchange."
- "I don't want to receive fifteen emails or texts a day telling me everything I do wrong as a parent."
- I don't want to destroy our children's childhood experience because we can't stop arguing."
- "I don't want to have our kids worried about where their mom and dad will sit on their wedding day."
- "I don't want to fight anymore."

Setting and implementing boundaries requires you to first figure out what you do want/need, like:

- "I need to feel safe in my home knowing the other parenting isn't going to walk in unannounced."
- "I want our children to be well-adjusted adults."
- "I need to create effective communication strategies to ensure our children's needs are always met."
- "I need to be less angry/anxious."

Once you figure out what you want/need, then and only then, can you create your boundaries.

THE BOUNDARY IS AN ACTION YOU NEED TO PUT INTO PLACE TO PROTECT YOU AND YOUR KIDS FROM A, B OR C.

The Implementation is the follow through you must do once you have created a boundary. You must follow the boundary you created. If you slip, even once, your boundary will be discredited by your co-parent and not followed.

The *follow through* is the knowledge that you will create a consequence when a boundary has been implemented but not followed.

The *consequence* is the action or outcome of violating the boundary. Most of us know that creating a consequence for a boundary not followed is almost harder than creating the boundary. High-conflict co-parents don't do boundaries and consequences because the rules don't apply to them. Make sure you create consequences you know you can follow through.

Creating boundaries will do nothing to move your situation forward if you do not implement them 100%. This is why it's vital that you fully understand your wants and needs. You will have greater power (willpower) to follow through on the boundaries you have created if you are clear on why you created them in the first place.

"IF YOU NEVER HEAL FROM WHAT HURT YOU, YOU'LL BLEED ON PEOPLE WHO DIDN'T CUT YOU."

—UNKNOWN

FEELINGS TO MOVE
- [ ] All of them (for clarity)

QUESTIONS
1. What don't you want?
2. What do you want?
3. What boundaries do you need to implement to get what you want?

CHALLENGE

This week we challenge you to go to bed one hour earlier than you normally do.

TAKE CARE CHECKLIST
- [ ] How much sleep are you getting?
- [ ] How often do you get into nature?
- [ ] Have you taken a bath, Jacuzzi or sauna?
- [ ] Have you completed the Trigger Challenge?
- [ ] Are you spending time with friends?
- [ ] When was the last time you read a book for pleasure?
- [ ] Have you taken a walk recently?
- [ ] How often do you move your body?
- [ ] Are you eating well?
- [ ] Do you mediate? Yoga?

PROGRESS CHECK-IN

TAKING CARE OF ME

3 ACTIVITIES outside my norm that improved my mood

1. ....

2. ....

3. ....

IMPROVING MY CO-PARENTING

3 STEPS I took to improve my co-parenting situation

1. ....

2. ....

3. ....

PROGRESS TO MAKE

1 SITUATION in which I could have done better with my co-parent or my kids

....

....

MY SUCESSES

1 SITUATION I did well and I'm proud of

....

....

REMINDERS

- ☐ Didn't take my frustration out on my kids
- ☐ Said something positive to my kids about their other parent, new partner, or grandparents (other family)
- ☐ Didn't yell at my kids
- ☐ BIFF'D all my written messages before sending them to my co-parent
- ☐ Reminded myself that I've got this!
- ☐ Reminded myself daily that I'm the only one who can manage my own emotions and behaviors

GOALS FOR NEXT MONTH

MY JOURNAL

INVISIBLE

It wasn't until recently that I understood what I was doing when faced with conflict. It wasn't until recently that I pieced together that my flexible thinking in the outside world was actually black and white thinking in my inside world.

It wasn't until recently that my inner world imploded and I realized that my response pattern, when faced with conflict, was to make myself invisible.

It seemed there was a mechanism in my brain that thought if I could just disappear, that I'd find my calm and peaceful world.

I gained weight (or lost weight). I would stop taking on clients (or take on too many). I would volunteer for everything (or remove myself from everything). I went from wearing pink to wearing all black (and sometimes beige).

I would try and blend. Blend in with whomever or whatever was going on around me. Because if I blended in, maybe the conflict wouldn't keep finding me.

And what does Dr Seuss say? "Why fit in when you were born to stand out."

But standing out was scary. Standing out, using my voice, being noticed? That all came with even more criticisms and I just needed the criticisms to stop. I needed to not make waves, to not attract any attention to myself, to not feel the pressure of any more conflict in my life.

So I did what I thought would make me safe—I made myself invisible. But when you make yourself invisible when you were meant to stand out, other negative things happen—things that are even worse than the co-parenting conflict you are experiencing.

Your light begins to dim, your health begins to suffer and you withdraw into a miserable place inside your head. You begin to see all that is wrong with the world through a magnifying glass. You sleep more than you are awake. You retreat so far you become a shell of yourself. And you hate that shell. You feel fear of being seen and therefore judged and/or criticized, anger at your circumstances, worry about your kid's well-being and ungrounded by all of the chaos around you. So you make yourself invisible.

Recognizing the response pattern of making yourself invisible is a big step in shifting it. I've been living and doing this work for over a decade and I just happened upon this pattern recently. I'm taking steps to address and overcoming it and I hope you do, too.

FEELINGS TO MOVE

- ☐ Fear
- ☐ Anger
- ☐ Worry
- ☐ Ungrounded

"THE MORE CHANCES YOU GIVE SOMEONE THE LESS RESPECT THEY'LL START TO HAVE FOR YOU. THEY'LL BEGIN TO IGNORE THE STANDARDS THAT YOU'VE SET BECAUSE THEY'LL KNOW ANOTHER CHANCE WILL ALWAYS BE GIVEN. THEY'RE NOT AFRAID TO LOSE YOU BECAUSE THEY KNOW NO MATTER WHAT YOU WON'T WALK AWAY. THEY GET COMFORTABLE WITH DEPENDING ON YOUR FORGIVENESS. NEVER LET A PERSON GET COMFORTABLE DISRESPECTING YOU."

—TRENT SHELTON

QUESTIONS

1. How have you made yourself invisible?
2. Who has noticed that you've made yourself invisible?
3. How has being invisible benefited you?

CHALLENGE

This week we challenge you to do 15 burpee's a day. For 7 days.

TAKE CARE CHECKLIST

- ☐ How much sleep are you getting?
- ☐ How often do you get into nature?
- ☐ Have you taken a bath, Jacuzzi or sauna?
- ☐ Have you completed the Trigger Challenge?
- ☐ Are you spending time with friends?
- ☐ When was the last time you read a book for pleasure?
- ☐ Have you taken a walk recently?
- ☐ How often do you move your body?
- ☐ Are you eating well?
- ☐ Do you mediate? Yoga?

SIMPLE

I know what you're thinking—that there is nothing simple about your co-parenting relationship. I'm not suggesting that it is simple. In fact, the mere reading of this survival guide tells me for certain that your co-parenting relationship is so complicated you can barely breathe most days.

You are hanging on by a thread, a frayed thread. Most days you don't know if you or your children are going to be safe in one way or another. Your mind races with thoughts about the difficulties understanding the laws and deciding what you're going to do, or as we've looked in past weeks, wondering how it happened to you and how do you make it stop.

And. And. And.

But the more your mind races, even more complicated questions keep coming up, which just make your mind race even more. You think that if you could just think of an option that hasn't been thought of yet, you might be able to fix this, calm this, reduce the mess of this, and navigate this co-parenting gig better.

Instead, everything just gets messier, more chaotic, and complicated beyond belief. It feels like your life has become a horror movie that you don't remember signing up for.

If going down the mental mind race rabbit hole is your response pattern, you are keeping yourself stuck by trying to control something that is out of your control.

WE CONTROL WHEN WE FEEL OUT OF CONTROL.

But your life is out of control. Your life is complicated. Your life is not simple.

But what if the answers to all of those complicated questions you keep asking are simple?

Before you roll your eyes at me, just hear me out. You can't change the past or predict the future, right? All you can do is breathe into the present moment wherever you may be. Did you just throw up a little in your mouth? Does it feel like I just told a terminally ill person the old adage that everything happens for a reason? Yes it probably does but don't worry, that's not what I meant by it.

When you strip away every complicated story you tell yourself, every story your co-parent tells you about yourself, every internal and external influence over your thoughts and feelings, what are you left with?

When you peel away all the labels you've given yourself (mom, wife, girlfriend, dad, husband, boyfriend, employee, president of xyz company, volunteer, home-maker, athlete etc) what are you left with?

FEELINGS TO MOVE

☐ Fear
☐ Anger
☐ Over Excitement
☐ Ungrounded
☐ Worry

YOU'RE LEFT WITH YOUR BREATH

Your breath is your love of self.

How often do you manage to find your breathe? I'm guessing never. Who has time to breathe? Thank heavens our bodies do it automatically! And if you aren't finding your breath, you aren't finding your self-love.

When your questions are complicated, your answers are simple. **Breathe.**

QUESTIONS

1. How can you implement simple into your complicated life?
2. What does simple look like?
3. How has a complicated life benefited you?

CHALLENGE

This week we challenge you to de-clutter your kitchen. Every cupboard, the counters and the fridge.

"ONE STEP AT A TIME. START BY DOING 1 PUSHUP. START BY DRINKING 1 CUP OF WATER. START BY PAYING TOWARD 1 DEBT. START BY READING 1 PAGE. START BY DELETING 1 OLD CONTACT. START BY WALKING 1 LAP. START BY WRITING 1 PARAGRAPH. JUST START."

—MINDFULNESS MATTERS

TAKE CARE CHECKLIST

☐ How much sleep are you getting?
☐ How often do you get into nature?
☐ Have you taken a bath, Jacuzzi or sauna?
☐ Have you completed the Trigger Challenge?
☐ Are you spending time with friends?
☐ When was the last time you read a book for pleasure?
☐ Have you taken a walk recently?
☐ How often do you move your body?
☐ Are you eating well?
☐ Do you mediate? Yoga?

HAPPY

It's hard to be happy when the energy of hate and misery are being forced upon you ALL. THE. TIME. It's also hard to be happy when it's such a broadly defined (or may it's not really defined at all) mysterious feeling.

We look at our friends who appear happy and try to be like them. Or we watch movies where the characters present happy so we try to be like them. We see strangers laughing and smiling on the street and assume they must be happy. But what is really happening when we're watching other people act happy? We're comparing ourselves to them, but we're not comparing ourselves to their reality—we're comparing ourselves to what they are presenting to the world. What they are presenting appears to be the elusive happiness you've been seeking.

But happiness isn't laughter. Or joke-telling. Or drinks with co-workers and friends. Happiness isn't something you can seek out; instead, it's something you create within.

Marilyn Monroe. Whitney Houston. Phillip Seymour Hoffman. Robin Williams.

All four of these personalities presented as what society stereotypically see as happy, yet all four succumbed to drug addiction and/or depression. If you continue to try and look for happiness outside yourself, your response pattern of giving up your power will continue to rob you of the happiness you are seeking.

Co-parenting with someone high-conflict pushes you into a state of external comparison. Comparison (competing) with anyone is the kiss of eternal unhappiness.

Happiness is elusive, 1000%, but it's not because your life circumstances are so challenging right now. It's because you aren't looking in the right place for it.

Genuine happiness, not the laughing joke-telling happiness, but the real peaceful and blissful happiness is a connection between the mind and the heart. I know this sounds woo-woo, but stick with me. When was the last time your head and heart felt connected? I'm guessing it's been awhile. Co-parenting with an HCP puts an electric fence with armed guards around our heart so no one can get in and with a guarded heart your feelings have nowhere to go so they become thoughts in your head.

Unfelt feelings become thoughts in your head.

Feelings, when felt, can pass. No one feeling sticks around for long if it's given the opportunity to be felt. But with a guarded heart, you're not feeling any feelings, at least not thoroughly. So the feelings move up to your head and you start over-thinking, and over-thinking makes you think you are feeling a feeling but it's just an illusion. Your brain attaches a story to your thinking and that story is given a feeling. So the story in your head is having feelings but your heart isn't.

Well that was complicated. It felt complicated to write too!

FEELINGS TO MOVE

☐ All of them

QUESTIONS

1. When was the last time you felt happy?
2. How do you define happy?
3. How has not being happy benefited you?

Your path to genuine happiness is through connecting your brain and your heart. Remove the armed guards around your heart and let the feelings roll in. The discomfort feels like it will last a lifetime, but it won't. Set a timer. I bet any given feeling that rolls in, if fully felt, won't last longer than five minutes.

Your internal happiness is worth five minutes.

CHALLENGE

This week we challenge you to find a way to laugh, hysterically. Spend time with a funny friend or colleague, watch a Netflix comedy special. Anything will as long as you find a way to laugh.

"YOUR NEED FOR ACCEPTANCE CAN MAKE YOU INVISIBLE IN THIS WORLD... RISK BEING SEEN IN ALL YOUR GLORY."

—JIM CAREY

TAKE CARE CHECKLIST

☐ How much sleep are you getting?
☐ How often do you get into nature?
☐ Have you taken a bath, Jacuzzi or sauna?
☐ Have you completed the Trigger Challenge?
☐ Are you spending time with friends?
☐ When was the last time you read a book for pleasure?
☐ Have you taken a walk recently?
☐ How often do you move your body?
☐ Are you eating well?
☐ Do you mediate? Yoga?

PERMISSION

You probably can't pinpoint exactly when it happened (neither can I in my own situation), but somewhere along the way you gave up your decision-making abilities and started looking for permission.

The law put some pressure on you to ask permission to:

- Put your kids in activities
- Travel
- Take your kids to the dentist
- Volunteer at school during your co-parent's parenting time
- Or to the eye-doctor
- Or the pediatrician
- Or even to your parents home.

But along the way you started believing you needed permission to do just about anything and everything. Permission to:

- Buy a new car
- Travel without your kids
- Buy a couch.

When the internal push to receive permission to live your life exists, your response pattern of giving away your power continues to control your life.

You are co-parenting; therefore, you are contractually obliged to make child-related decisions together (I know, as if that actually happens—but it's written down somewhere on a legal piece of paper that say it should happen). Decision-making is different from permission. Decision-making is mutual—permission is solitary. Decision-making is empowering—permission is submissive.

Decision-making with a high-conflict co-parent is riddled with challenges, but it is possible. This online course (New Ways for Families® Online: Parenting Without Conflict®: https://www.newways4families.com/pwc/) is a good place to learn how to handle decision-making with a high-conflict co-parent.

But non-child related decisions? None of anyone's business but your own! Your co-parent will try and make your personal, non-child related decisions about them and then they'll try to control your personal decisions. Suddenly you find yourself in a position where you're asking for their permission to change the locks on the house or put winter tires on your car or go away for the weekend without the kids.

You rationalize asking their permission. You think that if you give them perceived control over your personal decisions maybe they'll stop harassing you as aggressively as they have been.

But as the days, weeks and years go by of continuously asking permission to live your life, you've lost yourself. You've become afraid to make any decision without consult for fear of making the wrong decision.

We're told that there is no wrong decision but there is with a high-conflict co-parent. You have a long history of being told that every decision you have ever made is a wrong one.

So you ask permission.

News flash! It doesn't matter if you make a personal decision on your own or ask permission, your co-parent is going to find fault in you and your actions regardless.

It's time to take your power back.

"DIRECTION IS SO MUCH MORE IMPORTANT THAN SPEED. MANY ARE GOING NOWHERE FAST."

—UNKNOWN

FEELINGS TO MOVE
☐ All of them

QUESTIONS
1. What are you not doing for fear of not getting permission?
2. How has asking permission hindered your present state?
3. How has waiting to ask for permission benefited you?

CHALLENGE
This week we challenge you to do something without asking permission.

TAKE CARE CHECKLIST
☐ How much sleep are you getting?
☐ How often do you get into nature?
☐ Have you taken a bath, Jacuzzi or sauna?
☐ Have you completed the Trigger Challenge?
☐ Are you spending time with friends?
☐ When was the last time you read a book for pleasure?
☐ Have you taken a walk recently?
☐ How often do you move your body?
☐ Are you eating well?
☐ Do you mediate? Yoga?

PROGRESS CHECK-IN

TAKING CARE OF ME

3 ACTIVITIES outside my norm that improved my mood

1. _____

2. _____

3. _____

IMPROVING MY CO-PARENTING

3 STEPS I took to improve my co-parenting situation

1. _____

2. _____

3. _____

PROGRESS TO MAKE

1 SITUATION in which I could have done better with my co-parent or my kids

_____

_____

MY SUCESSES

1 SITUATION I did well and I'm proud of

_____

_____

REMINDERS

☐ Didn't take my frustration out on my kids

☐ Said something positive to my kids about their other parent, new partner, or grandparents (other family)

☐ Didn't yell at my kids

☐ BIFF'D all my written messages before sending them to my co-parent

☐ Reminded myself that I've got this!

☐ Reminded myself daily that I'm the only one who can manage my own emotions and behaviors

GOALS FOR NEXT MONTH

MY JOURNAL

SELF-LOVE

Love yourself and everything will be okay. That lip service is enough to make you want to hit someone when you're involved in high-conflict co-parenting.

But that's just because you don't understand it because **self-love is elusive.** We can assume that a majority of people never experience it while the rest can't figure out how to articulate how to find it.

You eat well. You work out. You try to do good. That's self-love, right? **No.**

You shower daily(ish), make time for friends and family and see a therapist. That's self-love, right? **No.**

Those are all self-care activities, which are needed to help you get to self-love. But they aren't self-love.

SELF-LOVE IS NON-JUDGEMENT OF SELF

Now do you see why it's so elusive?

Have you ever gone an hour, let alone five minutes, without that little voice in your head judging you in some way? My little voice can be mean and nasty.

- It compares me to others.
- It tells me I'm not good enough.
- It tells me I'm fat.
- It tells me I'm a fraud.
- It tells me I'm a bad mom.
- It tells me to do more.
- It tells me receiving goodness and positivity is bad.

That little voice in my head? That judgmental one? That's self-hatred at its finest. What does your little voice say to you?

I'm guessing it mimics what your co-parent says to you. Verbatim.

You're hearing from the itty, bitty, shitty committee judging you not once , but twice? Your high-conflict co-parent and your inner little voice? No wonder you can't get yourself to the elusive self-love! You probably just judged yourself for not being able to get there, didn't you?

That self-judgmental voice is a doozy of a response pattern. The voice was created to keep you safe from the possibility of an awesome life full of adventure because the voice is terrified of change. The voice is terrified you might find self-love because if you find self-love then you might not listen to the voice anymore.

But now you know it's there.

And now you can call it out for what it's doing, mimicking the words of your high-conflict co-parents' judgments because it thinks that's how it can keep you safe. Safe from what? Usually feelings. The voice hates feelings so it keeps you safe and small to keep you from learning that feelings aren't that scary.

True safety? Self-love.
True self-love? Non-judgement of self.

The next time you hear the voice in your head judging you, catch it and call it out. "No judgement, thanks. I'm working on self-love."

Sounds corny, but it works. Try it.
What have you got to lose?

"MY BIGGEST MISTAKES IN LIFE HAVE ALL STEMMED FROM GIVING MY POWER TO SOMEONE ELSE— BELIEVING THAT THE LOVE OTHERS HAD TO OFFER WAS MORE IMPORTANT THAN THE LOVE I HAD TO GIVE TO MYSELF."

—OPRAH WINFREY

"THE HARDEST PART OF BEING STRONG IS THAT NO ONE EVER ASKS IF YOU'RE OKAY."

—UNKNOWN

FEELINGS TO MOVE
☐ All of them

QUESTIONS
1. How do you define self-love?
2. When was the last time you felt self-love?
3. How can you teach your kids to love themselves?

CHALLENGE
Write 10 things about yourself that you love, every day, for 7 days.

TAKE CARE CHECKLIST
☐ How much sleep are you getting?
☐ How often do you get into nature?
☐ Have you taken a bath, Jacuzzi or sauna?
☐ Have you completed the Trigger Challenge?
☐ Are you spending time with friends?
☐ When was the last time you read a book for pleasure?
☐ Have you taken a walk recently?
☐ How often do you move your body?
☐ Are you eating well?
☐ Do you mediate? Yoga?

NUMB

Have you found yourself staring out window at nothing in particular with a blank mind and a blank heart? Or do you find yourself going through the actions of life putting a smile on your face when it's appropriate but not feeling the joy that you have splattered all over your face?

Have you lost your ability to cry? To laugh? Do you feel angry all the time? Or terrified? Or maybe you feel absolutely nothing at all?

When a feeling does arise, do you reach for food to squash it? Wine to calm it? Netflix to distract it? Or do you retreat to your inner world that no one else knows exists and just hover there?

ARE YOU NUMB?

You don't intentionally make yourself numb. You just think that if one more whammy is directed at you and you let yourself feel it, whatever that feeling may be, that you won't survive. The next attack or threat will be the one that breaks the camel's back. That camel is you.

If your response pattern is to numb whatever feeling may be trying to escape, then you have created a life of self-protection and guardedness. You numb yourself to get through the day, waiting for nightfall so you can go to bed because your co-parent can't hurt you when you're sleeping. You hit snooze on your alarm clock five times to avoid the day and what might be thrown at you from your co-parent. Or you jump out of bed to check your phone to see how many emails or texts they sent so you can stay ahead of the day and its potential threats.

Being numb seems like it is a far easier way to survive life when you're co-parenting with someone who presents as high-conflict, but if you're numbing to survive your life, then you aren't living your life.

"But I can't live my life," you say, or "My co-parent has created a whole world where I am the puppet and she/he is the master and if I don't do what the master says, the master will up their game playing and I will crumble." Because you can't take anymore. You're barely hanging on.

So you numb.

But numbing has its side effects. Perverse, penetrating and persistent side effects like sleep disturbances, unexplained aches and pains, strained friendships, weight loss/gain, poor productivity at work and at home. Numbing the pain and anger and terror you have been feeling around co-parenting with your children's other parent continues to prevent you from feeling and experiencing life to its fullest.

Feelings are life. When there are no feelings, there is no life.

Let's swing the pendulum the other way, from numb to feeling, and let's get you your life back.

"EMBRACE UNCERTAINTY. SOME OF THE MOST BEAUTIFUL CHAPTERS OF OUR LIVES WON'T HAVE A TITLE UNTIL MUCH LATER."

—POSITIVITY LOVER

FEELINGS TO MOVE
- ☐ Anger
- ☐ Fear
- ☐ Surrender
- ☐ Excessive Giddiness
- ☐ Worry

QUESTIONS
1. How have you numbed yourself?
2. What benefit are you getting from numbing?
3. What would it look like if you weren't numb?

CHALLENGE
This week we challenge you to show up in your life. Every time you feel the need to numb or isolate, remind yourself to show up.

TAKE CARE CHECKLIST
- ☐ How much sleep are you getting?
- ☐ How often do you get into nature?
- ☐ Have you taken a bath, Jacuzzi or sauna?
- ☐ Have you completed the Trigger Challenge?
- ☐ Are you spending time with friends?
- ☐ When was the last time you read a book for pleasure?
- ☐ Have you taken a walk recently?
- ☐ How often do you move your body?
- ☐ Are you eating well?
- ☐ Do you mediate? Yoga?

ANGER

Anger is an interesting word. A vague word. While it's almost universally used to describe a feeling, it's hard to pinpoint exactly what the definition of angry is. Generally anger is defined as intense, uncomfortable response to feeling like you're under threat or being hurt.

That sounds more like rage to me, not anger.

Anger feels like a low-grade fever, just hovering there, feeling uncomfortable but not out of control.

Rage is an intense expression of emotion, not anger. Anger is a culmination of disappointment, discouragement, mistrust, hurt, doubt, bewilderment, loss, frustration, unjustness, shock, guilt, shame, bitterness and disbelief, to name a few. While anger appears to be the go-to word for any uncomfortable feelings, it shouldn't be feared the way rage is. And it shouldn't be avoided.

We've become neutralized to the word anger and toss it around in casual conversation without any regard for its actual definition.

"He/She is so angry all the time."
"She/He has anger issues or a bad temper."
"He/She is just an angry person."

When did we start defining people with the emotions they feel? For years I was a self-described angry person. It was the rhetoric I spoke when someone asked me about myself. Twisted, I know, but at the time I didn't know any better.

For some, instead of neutralizing the word anger, they start to fear it.

"She is scared of her co-parent's anger."
"He cowers to her angry emails."

If we take the time to understand what anger is rather than attaching a story to what anger means, the power of the word anger diminishes.

My definition of anger: It's a feeling. Anger is a feeling.

When you feel anger or are in the physical space with someone who is feeling angry, rather than attach a story to the anger, just feel it. This is easier said than done because our brains want to immediately attach a story to the uncomfortable feeling.

If your response pattern is to attach a story to anger, yours or your co-parents, then you are allowing your brain to trump your heart. Your heart just wants to feel the anger and move it. Your brain wants to understand it and fix it so that it never happens again.

But like all feelings, anger isn't permanent. Your brain is wrong in its attempts to fix the anger so that it won't happen again. Anger will always happen again. Because feelings happen. Because life is feelings. If feelings stop, you die.

Instead of trying to fix the anger, try feeling the anger. From the top of your skull right now to the tips of your toes. Feel it for a solid 5 minutes. Set a timer. Keep all storytelling out of it, just feel it. It's going to be gross and uncomfortable because it's new for you. Do it anyway.

"MASTERING OTHERS IS STRENGTH. MASTERING YOURSELF IS TRUE POWER."

—LAO TZU

FEELINGS TO MOVE

☐ Fear
☐ Worry
☐ Anger

QUESTIONS

1. How does your anger present itself?
2. What benefit are you getting from staying angry?
3. How do your kids display their anger?

CHALLENGE

This week we challenge you to throw a 30-second tantrum in your room every day. Set a timer and let her rip. Scream, punch pillows, stomp your feet. Throw a wicked tantrum for 30 seconds.

TAKE CARE CHECKLIST

☐ How much sleep are you getting?
☐ How often do you get into nature?
☐ Have you taken a bath, Jacuzzi or sauna?
☐ Have you completed the Trigger Challenge?
☐ Are you spending time with friends?
☐ When was the last time you read a book for pleasure?
☐ Have you taken a walk recently?
☐ How often do you move your body?
☐ Are you eating well?
☐ Do you mediate? Yoga?

BLISS

Bliss is that magical place where your head and your heart are 100% connected and it feels like regardless of what is happening around you, you feel like anything is possible. My favorite feeling in the whole wide world? The possibility of possibility. For me, that's nirvana.

Bliss sounds like it should be an easy thing to achieve. Connect the head and the heart and voilà—bliss. But it's far from easy and requires work, dedication and trust. Trust?

Co-parenting with a high-conflict personality can be excruciating (and I don't use that word lightly). You've been emotionally tossed around like a bean bag in a game of hot potato. You have felt angry, sad, lost, frustrated, in shock and terrified. But bliss? Nah, that feeling has been evasive.

HOW CAN YOU FEEL BLISS WHILE BEING HARASSED, MANIPULATED, LIED TO, CHEATED ON AND CONTROLLED?

All caps used for emphasis. If someone had told me that bliss was possible while still managing the relationship with the high-conflict person in my life I would have yelled at them. Seriously! How can anyone feel bliss, the feeling of possibility, when your whole existence seems impossible to escape from?

If your response pattern is to believe that feeling bliss has to wait until the chaos of your life slows down, then you are allowing external debris to influence your internal world.

Your head: The voice, your ego, the rational brain, the fixer personality, the story teller.

Your heart: the place in which you feel all your feelings.

Bliss: That magical place where your head and your heart merge, where your feelings and your thoughts connect as one, and you begin trust in what is possible.

Your co-parent will never change. I can almost 100% guarantee that. **But you can.**

If you genuinely want to feel your Bliss and are willing to put in the work to help your heart learn to feel and your head learn to let go, then your possibilities are endless. The path to Bliss ebbs and flows. Some days are easier than others. Stay the course. In time, when you have learned to continuously feel your feelings, the ebbs get shorter and the flows get longer. Bliss is not the proverbial Unicorn. It is not saved for the rich and famous, nor the super evolved Mother Theresa and Ghandi's of the world.

Bliss is for anyone who is willing to connect their heads with their hearts.

"SOMETIMES YOU NEED TO CHANGE THE PLAN, NOT THE GOAL."

—MEL ROBBINS

FEELINGS TO MOVE
☐ All of them

QUESTIONS
1. When was the last time you felt bliss?
2. What is preventing you from feeling bliss right now?
3. What choices can you make, today, to ensure you feel bliss every day?

CHALLENGE
This week we challenge you to find a park bench and just sit on it for 15 minutes. Don't check your phone, don't think about your co-parent. Look at the people going by and be curious about how they find their bliss. 15 minutes. Park bench. 3x.

TAKE CARE CHECKLIST
☐ How much sleep are you getting?
☐ How often do you get into nature?
☐ Have you taken a bath, Jacuzzi or sauna?
☐ Have you completed the Trigger Challenge?
☐ Are you spending time with friends?
☐ When was the last time you read a book for pleasure?
☐ Have you taken a walk recently?
☐ How often do you move your body?
☐ Are you eating well?
☐ Do you mediate? Yoga?

PROGRESS CHECK-IN

TAKING CARE OF ME

3 ACTIVITIES outside my norm that improved my mood

1. _____

2. _____

3. _____

IMPROVING MY CO-PARENTING

3 STEPS I took to improve my co-parenting situation

1. _____

2. _____

3. _____

PROGRESS TO MAKE

1 SITUATION in which I could have done better with my co-parent or my kids

_____

_____

_____

MY SUCESSES

1 SITUATION I did well and I'm proud of

_____

_____

_____

REMINDERS

☐ Didn't take my frustration out on my kids

☐ Said something positive to my kids about their other parent, new partner, or grandparents (other family)

☐ Didn't yell at my kids

☐ BIFF'D all my written messages before sending them to my co-parent

☐ Reminded myself that I've got this!

☐ Reminded myself daily that I'm the only one who can manage my own emotions and behaviors

GOALS FOR NEXT MONTH

MY JOURNAL

TERROR

Generally speaking, I think it's hard to describe terror to someone who has never felt it before. If your blood has never gone cold simply because an email has popped into your inbox from your co-parent, how can you possibly understand terror? If you have never left a squeaky bedroom door squeaky because it gave you comfort in knowing you might wake up if someone tries to enter your bedroom, how can you possibly understand terror?

If you've never felt the utter shock of having your children, the beings you love more than anything in this world, told horrific lies about you, how can you possibly understand terror?

If you've never sat in a room, not knowing if the Judge/Mediator/Arbitrator/Parenting Coordinator (or whichever professional you are using) believed your co-parent's lies and will be changing the parenting plan to correlate to their lies, how could you possibly understand terror?

If you've never avoided going out past dark, for fear of who might be following you, how could you possibly understand terror?

I know, without a shadow of a doubt, that if you are co-parenting with someone who has high-conflict personality tendencies that you know terror. You have experienced terror. You have felt terror in the depths of your soul, and that it was one of the scariest feelings you have ever felt and possibly continue to feel.

Terror itself is not a response pattern. Choosing to stay in terror is. Choosing to stay in terror allows the external world to control your personal world.

Moving terror is not easy because it's hard to pinpoint exactly where we are holding it in our bodies and brains. It's a pervasive feeling that hovers in our psyche and our physical being and sometimes it's there and we don't even know it's there, because we have other response patterns in place to mask its presence.

Unacknowledged terror often presents itself in the body as uncontrollable, involuntary shaking. Almost like when you are shivering in the cold? But it's not cold. If you have ever found your body involuntarily shaking without any perceived reason, it's shaking to remove the overabundance of terror it's been holding.

Your goal is to not let the terror accumulate to such an extent that your body shakes on its own. You want to move the terror your body is holding every day (or hour to start, depending on the severity of the terror) so that you don't get stuck in terror.

When you are in terror, you are vulnerable to control and manipulations. When you move the terror, you reclaim your power and are less susceptible to negative influences outside your control.

> **"A SHIP IN THE HARBOR IS SAFE, BUT THAT IS NOT WHAT SHIPS ARE BUILT FOR."**
>
> —JOHN A SHEDD

> **"THE SIX BEST DOCTORS IN THE WORLD ARE SUNLIGHT, REST, EXERCISE, DIET, SELF-CONFIDENCE AND FRIENDS. MAINTAIN THEM IN ALL STAGES AND ENJOY A HEALTHY LIFE."**
>
> —STEVE JOBS

FEELINGS TO MOVE
☐ Fear

QUESTIONS
1. What are you most afraid of?
2. How has that fear prevented you from being the parent you wished you could be?
3. How would you parent if you weren't afraid?

CHALLENGE
This week we challenge you to do three 15-minute yoga lessons (easy to find on YouTube).

TAKE CARE CHECKLIST
☐ How much sleep are you getting?
☐ How often do you get into nature?
☐ Have you taken a bath, Jacuzzi or sauna?
☐ Have you completed the Trigger Challenge?
☐ Are you spending time with friends?
☐ When was the last time you read a book for pleasure?
☐ Have you taken a walk recently?
☐ How often do you move your body?
☐ Are you eating well?
☐ Do you mediate? Yoga?

MOURNING

In order to live the life you are meant to live, you need to mourn the life you thought you'd have. No one ever dreams of co-parenting with a high-conflict person. Not ever.

No one romanticizes a 50/50 parenting schedule, alternating holidays with your kids, asking for permission to travel or having to spend a thousand dollars on mediation to figure out who can make a dentist appointment. No one plans for their future to filled with lies, manipulations and control by the person they had a child(ren) with.

So, when an experience such as the horrific one you're having takes over your life, you dig your heals in and you fight back. You do everything you can to fix what is broken. You hold onto a dream of what could be if you could just see eye-to-eye. You begin to hyper-control the language in your parenting plan (we control when we feel out of control), you research articles on how to co-parent more effectively, and you put your whole life on hold until you figure this out and make it better.

But it's not going to get better. In fact, it might even get worse. I'm not saying that to depress you further, I'm trying to wake you up to your reality. If your co-parent has high-conflict tendencies, the likelihood that they will one day wake up and get it or change or want to be amicable is zero. Your co-parent will never change. Never, ever, ever.

Until you mourn that the possibility for your co-parent to change isn't an option, you will keep spinning your wheels trying to fix the present, which will only continue to cause you anguish in your future.

Mourning what could have been allows you to end a chapter in your life that is no longer serving you. It will feel like you aren't fighting for your kids, like you are giving up. That's just the story the voice is telling you to keep you stuck in your response pattern of fighting for the dream you want to believe is possible.

The cycle of grief kicks in when you try to mourn what could have been and you may find yourself bargaining with mourning rather than just letting it flow. Or getting angry with the fact that you have to mourn at all. Why do you have to do all the work and your co-parent can just keep being miserable and awful? Or, when the mourning gets too hard, you deny that it needs to happen at all, and instead you jump back in to trying to fix an unfixable problem.

Accepting the loss of the life you could have had, the life your kids could have had, will open the door to the possibility of a life far greater.

"FOCUS ON YOU FOR A CHANGE: STOP WORRYING ABOUT OTHER PEOPLE UNDERSTANDING YOU. GET IN TOUCH WITH YOURSELF INSTEAD. FOCUS ON WHAT MAKES YOU HAPPY, WHAT MAKES YOUR SOUL FEEL AT PEACE. YOU ARE YOUR BIGGEST COMMITMENT, SO START LOVING YOUR FLAWS, YOUR AWKWARDNESS, YOUR WEIRDNESS, YOUR INTENSITY, YOUR VULNERABILITY, YOUR EVERYTHING. LIFE BECOMES SO MUCH MORE FULFILLING WHEN YOU ARE JUST SIMPLY YOURSELF. THE WORLD KEEPS SPINNING WHETHER PEOPLE UNDERSTAND YOU OR NOT, SO WHY NOT MAKE THIS NEXT TRIP AROUND THE SUN ABOUT YOU."

—VYBE SOURCE

FEELINGS TO MOVE
☐ Surrender

QUESTIONS
1. Have you mourned the loss of the life you thought you'd have?
2. Have you mourned the loss of the life you thought your kids would have?
3. Have you created a model in your brain with how your life could be awesome even though you are co-parenting with the devil?

CHALLENGE
Our challenge to you this week is to create a vision board on how your life could look from today moving forward, regardless of what obstacles your co-parent puts in your path.

TAKE CARE CHECKLIST
☐ How much sleep are you getting?
☐ How often do you get into nature?
☐ Have you taken a bath, Jacuzzi or sauna?
☐ Have you completed the Trigger Challenge?
☐ Are you spending time with friends?
☐ When was the last time you read a book for pleasure?
☐ Have you taken a walk recently?
☐ How often do you move your body?
☐ Are you eating well?
☐ Do you mediate? Yoga?

UNCONDITIONAL
PART 1

What is unconditional love? Is it parents lovingly watching their kids play at the park, waving goodbye to their kids on the first day of school or mom and dad kissing a sleeping child. I don't think so.
But society has us believing it is.

My definition of **unconditional love:** 100% acceptance of who someone is (self-included) without judgement.

Stop trying to fix the unfixable to give your kids the childhood you thought you'd be giving them. They don't know what they are missing. All they know is the here and now of what they are living. Sure, it would be awesome for them to have amicable parents who can co-host Christmas or Hanukah together, but that's not their reality.

Sure, it would be awesome if both parents took them to their activities during their parenting time rather than using attendance as a tool to manipulate the other parent, but that's not their reality. Nor is it what they need to grow into healthy, emotionally competent adults.

So, what DO your kids need? Unconditional love. Unconditional love by one parent or other trusted adult in their life. One person who accepts them for who they are, for the feelings they feel, even when their behavior is hormonal and irrational—without judgement.

Reflect on how you've been parenting and how your co-parent has been parenting. Have either of you been loving your child(ren) unconditionally? Accepting them without judgement?

Often times, when trying to manage a high-conflict co-parent, we try to coach our kids to behave a certain way for fear that their other parent may criticize us for our parenting skills. Or:

- we coach our kids on how to behave in the other parent's home so that they don't get the tongue lashings and abuse that you got when you lived under their roof
- react out of fear or anger when the kids come home from their other parent's house and say awful things about us
- be so stressed out with trying to manage and fix all the 'problems' their co-parent throws at them they are short tempered and irritable with their kids.

Social media presents unconditional love in the form of happy, smiling families dressed in color coordinated outfits. Television gave us the Cosby Show, the picture-perfect family who easily resolved all of life's challenges with a joke and a hug (and we know how that ended).

UNCONDITIONAL LOVE IS NOT A FEELING—IT'S AN ACTION. ACCEPTANCE WITHOUT JUDGEMENT IS AN ACTION.

Your children don't need Christmas or Hanukah traditions repeated year after year and they won't be screwed up for life because their mom and dad don't get along, as long as you give them the one thing they do need—your unconditional love, your acceptance of who they are, how they behave and what they feel unconditionally.

"WE DON'T' WANT TO KNOW WHAT WE ALREADY KNOW."

—GENEEN ROTH

FEELINGS TO MOVE
☐ All of them

QUESTIONS
1. How do you define unconditional love?
2. How do you show your kids unconditional love?
3. Did you feel unconditional love as a child?

CHALLENGE
This week we challenge you to write 500 words on what you would want your children to say in regards to how they felt unconditional love when they are 25 years old.

TAKE CARE CHECKLIST
☐ How much sleep are you getting?
☐ How often do you get into nature?
☐ Have you taken a bath, Jacuzzi or sauna?
☐ Have you completed the Trigger Challenge?
☐ Are you spending time with friends?
☐ When was the last time you read a book for pleasure?
☐ Have you taken a walk recently?
☐ How often do you move your body?
☐ Are you eating well?
☐ Do you mediate? Yoga?

UNCONDITIONAL
PART 2

What is unconditional love of self? Internet writers have romanticized unconditional love into gift-giving, hand-holding and grand proposals.

My definition of **unconditional love of self:** 100% acceptance of who you are without judgement. Stop laughing, I'm serious. Many give lip service to self-love, dismissing its existence as being a given.

"Of course I love myself."

But loving yourself is different than unconditional self-love. It's the place of unconditional self-love where your freedom exists. You've been searching for your freedom for years, maybe even decades.

- If you could just get a decent parenting plan, the fighting would stop and you could be free.
- If you could just get the communication to improve, you'd be free.
- If the attacks and manipulations would just stop, you'd be free.

But you wouldn't be free, because your co-parent has high-conflict tendencies and once one issue is resolved they will just create a new one. Depending on something external to change in order to be free, to feel free, will ensure you will never find the freedom you are seeking.

True freedom is the exquisite power of knowing that regardless of what your external world is throwing at you, your internal world is complete with the unconditional love of self. It sounds like hocus pocus.

Like some woo woo, drug-inspired state of being that doesn't actually exist. But hear me out.

If you are being called a horrific parent who should have the kids removed from your care every day and you don't have the power of unconditional self-love bringing you back to reality, your ego will take over and start to believe the story it is being told. If your ego starts to believe the story it is being told, you begin to believe that maybe you aren't a great parent and your feelings of self-worth deteriorate. With low self-worth, controllers and manipulators have easier access to your inner world, forcing you into a world of self-hate.

Self-hate is full of judgement, conditional love and non-acceptance.

Unconditional self-love will be your only successful path to freedom.

When you accept without judgement all of your flaws, poor decisions and actions and all of your awesomeness, no one will be able to control or manipulate you. No one will be able to convince you that you're a terrible parent. No one will be able to steal your valuable time and energy with frivolous accusations and threats. No one will be able to take your freedom.

Because your freedom isn't found outside of you, it's found within.

FEELINGS TO MOVE
- [ ] All of them

QUESTIONS
1. Do you love yourself without judgement?
2. How has your lack of self-love benefited you?
3. What does unconditional self -love look like to you?

CHALLENGE
This week we challenge you to make a list of 10 judgements you make about yourself in your head. Then make a list beside each judgement on an activity you can do that judgement creeps back into your head.

TAKE CARE CHECKLIST
- [ ] How much sleep are you getting?
- [ ] How often do you get into nature?
- [ ] Have you taken a bath, Jacuzzi or sauna?
- [ ] Have you completed the Trigger Challenge?
- [ ] Are you spending time with friends?
- [ ] When was the last time you read a book for pleasure?
- [ ] Have you taken a walk recently?
- [ ] How often do you move your body?
- [ ] Are you eating well?
- [ ] Do you mediate? Yoga?

"SELF-LOVE WILL SAVE YOUR SOUL."
—R.H. SIN

PROGRESS CHECK-IN

TAKING CARE OF ME

3 ACTIVITIES outside my norm that improved my mood

1. _____

2. _____

3. _____

IMPROVING MY CO-PARENTING

3 STEPS I took to improve my co-parenting situation

1. _____

2. _____

3. _____

PROGRESS TO MAKE

1 SITUATION in which I could have done better with my co-parent or my kids

_____

_____

MY SUCESSES

1 SITUATION I did well and I'm proud of

_____

_____

REMINDERS

- ☐ Didn't take my frustration out on my kids
- ☐ Said something positive to my kids about their other parent, new partner, or grandparents (other family)
- ☐ Didn't yell at my kids
- ☐ BIFF'D all my written messages before sending them to my co-parent
- ☐ Reminded myself that I've got this!
- ☐ Reminded myself daily that I'm the only one who can manage my own emotions and behaviors

GOALS FOR NEXT MONTH

MY JOURNAL

BRAVE

If you are co-parenting with an HCP, it's possible you haven't felt brave in years. Every time you felt ready to be brave and put you first, and you put some time and energy into yourself rather than the nonstop conflict, another shoe drops.

You begin to wonder how many shoes can possibly drop before the whole floor collapses?

We think brave means feeling the fear of whatever scares us and doing it anyway. We think brave means standing up to bullies. We think brave means anything and everything we aren't. What is brave?

Is it that we are ready to show courage while facing danger? If this is true, then you've lived your whole co-parenting existence brave and you didn't even know it.

Each and every day that you wake up, you are being brave. Every day you wake up, you have no idea how the day will unfold. Not because you have a crazy life (everyone has a crazy life), but because you are co-parenting with someone who presents as unpredictable, chaotic and sometimes a little bit deranged.

And yet you don't feel brave.

But how does brave feel? Competent? Successful? Confident? Nah.

BRAVE IS:

- relief that you survived the day
- an extra 30 seconds in a day to breathe in deeply and exhale slowly
- responding instead of reacting, even if it was only once
- shutting your phone off for a full 24 hours
- not giving up, even when you really, really want to
- allowing yourself to cry
- taking an hour to get your nails done, get a massage, go for a run
- reading this survival guide, wanting to learn more, try harder and do better
- everything you're doing, right now.

And yet you don't feel brave. Why not? Because **brave isn't a feeling—it's an action.** Brave is doing anything and everything, regardless of how small or large.

As Brene Brown states, "Sometimes the bravest and most important thing you can do is just show up."

YOU ARE SHOWING UP.
YOU ARE BRAVE.

"SELF-CARE IS HOW YOU TAKE YOUR POWER BACK."

—LAW OF ATTRACTION

FEELINGS TO MOVE
☐ All of them

QUESTIONS
1. Do you feel brave?
2. What do you think needs to happen to feel brave?
3. How has not feeling brave benefited you?

CHALLENGE
This week we challenge you to do the Wonder Woman or Superman pose for 30 seconds each morning in the mirror. Put your hands on your hips, stick out your chest and pretend you're Wonder Woman or Superman. For 30 seconds.

TAKE CARE CHECKLIST
☐ How much sleep are you getting?
☐ How often do you get into nature?
☐ Have you taken a bath, Jacuzzi or sauna?
☐ Have you completed the Trigger Challenge?
☐ Are you spending time with friends?
☐ When was the last time you read a book for pleasure?
☐ Have you taken a walk recently?
☐ How often do you move your body?
☐ Are you eating well?
☐ Do you mediate? Yoga?

CULTIVATE

It's easy to describe what we don't like, what we don't want, what the feelings we despise. We hate the disrespect our co-parent shows us. We can't stand how tormented our kids are, feeling pulled back and forth like a game of tug-of-war. We are crushed that it feels like we have no say in how our children grow up or what they will have the opportunity to experience or not experience.

WE DON'T WANT:

- A 50/50 parenting schedule
- To share holiday days
- Our kids fed lies about us
- Email after email, text after text telling us how awful we are as a human, a parent, a colleague or friend
- To feel guilt and shame for trying to co-parent amicably and failing
- Exchanges to take place at police stations
- To feel terrified every time the children transition to their other parent's house
- To feel paralyzed when the phone rings
- To blame ourselves for the mess we're in
- This experience anymore.

WE WANT A REDO.

We can list off 1000 feelings or things we don't like but if your focus is always on what is wrong, what you don't like, what hate about your life, then your experience will continue to focus on all that is awful about your current circumstances.

"WHAT YOU FOCUS ON GROWS, WHAT YOU THINK ABOUT EXPANDS AND WHAT YOU DWELL UPON DETERMINES YOUR DESTINY."
—ROBIN S. SHARMA

Do you really want to expand the way you currently feel? Instead what if you focused on what you wanted your life to look like? What if you focused on what was good with your children? What if instead of thinking incessantly about what is bad, you flipped the switch and focused on the feelings you wish to be experiencing instead.

Do you know what feelings you want to be feeling? Start taking thirty seconds each day to focus on those feelings, and continue adding more time each day. Cultivate a tickle trunk full of feel good feelings you can pull from when you have a spare couple of seconds so you can practice. That way when life seems extra hard and challenging you have a memory of what a feel good feeling feels like and you can take a mental escape and feel that positive feeling—even if you have to fake it. Fake it till you make it!

What would those feel good feelings be? How would you express them? Where would you express them? Who would you share them with?

Cultivate Love. Cultivate Peace. Cultivate Quiet. Cultivate Adventure. Cultivate Easy. Cultivate Laughter. Cultivate Lightness. Cultivate Freedom.

Cultivate the experience inside your head that you want to be living regardless of the noise of the outside world.

"IT IS THROUGH GRATITUDE FOR THE PRESENT MOMENT THAT THE SPIRITUAL DIMENSION OF LIFE OPENS UP."

—ECKHART TOLLE

FEELINGS TO MOVE
☐ All of them

QUESTIONS
1. What experiences do you want to cultivate for yourself?
2. What experiences do you want to cultivate for your kids?
3. How can you make those happen?

CHALLENGE
This week we challenge you to cultivate a family dinner, prepped and cooked by everyone in your home. Is your youngest too small to sit up? Plop them in a bumbo and let them watch. No excuses, grab your family members and cultivate a meal together.

TAKE CARE CHECKLIST
☐ How much sleep are you getting?
☐ How often do you get into nature?
☐ Have you taken a bath, Jacuzzi or sauna?
☐ Have you completed the Trigger Challenge?
☐ Are you spending time with friends?
☐ When was the last time you read a book for pleasure?
☐ Have you taken a walk recently?
☐ How often do you move your body?
☐ Are you eating well?
☐ Do you mediate? Yoga?

FREEDOM

Does it feel like you have freedom? Do you feel empowered? Does it feel like you can act, speak or think without being criticized, ridiculed or demeaned?

Probably not; however, you know what it feels like to be controlled and stuck under the thumb of someone who creates drama faster than most of us can blink our eyes.

Freedom? You can't even travel without permission.

Freedom? You can't book a doctor's appointment without conflict.

Freedom? You can't ask for a trade in parenting time without world war three.

Your freedom is zilch. Non-existent.

But what if we tweaked the definition of freedom a little? What if instead of searching for freedom externally, searching for the external right to do something, we looked inwards instead? What if freedom wasn't something beyond your control, but something you created inside you?

"FREEDOM IS REALIZING YOU HAVE A CHOICE."
—T.F. HODGE

You can't choose to have the freedom of not co-parenting with your children's other parent nor can you choose to have the freedom of having your kids all the time, making all their decisions, choosing their diet, navigating their friends. And you can't choose how many emails are sent to you in any given day.

But you can choose to have freedom from the ups and downs of the emotions you are having.

YOU CAN CHOOSE:

- **to disengage** from constant electronic communications
- **to accept** that your external world is chaotic but your inner world doesn't need to be
- **to move through** your inner conflict rather than get stuck in it
- **to spend the time** you have with your kids present and engaged
- **to re-work** the life you thought you'd be living, mourn the loss, and choose how you're going to feel moving forward.

You can choose your freedom.

It's not going to look like how you thought freedom would look and that's okay. Your freedom is yours to create, internally. When we seek freedom from the external mayhem around us we get stuck in the spinning tornado and just end up becoming part of the destruction it left behind.

When we can create internal freedom, it doesn't matter where you are or who you're with or what is being said to you or about you. No one can take away the feeling of freedom within. And that kind of freedom? That's power. True, genuine, power.

FEELINGS TO MOVE
- ☐ Over-excited
- ☐ Anger
- ☐ Fear
- ☐ Worry
- ☐ Grief

QUESTIONS
1. What does freedom look like to you?
2. How does freedom feel?
3. What is preventing you from cultivating that feeling now?

CHALLENGE
This week we challenge you to disconnect from your phone, your computer, Facebook, Instagram, Snapchat – all technology. Disconnect from the outside word for a minimum of 12 hours a day. For 12 hours a day, give yourself freedom.

TAKE CARE CHECKLIST
- ☐ How much sleep are you getting?
- ☐ How often do you get into nature?
- ☐ Have you taken a bath, Jacuzzi or sauna?
- ☐ Have you completed the Trigger Challenge?
- ☐ Are you spending time with friends?
- ☐ When was the last time you read a book for pleasure?
- ☐ Have you taken a walk recently?
- ☐ How often do you move your body?
- ☐ Are you eating well?
- ☐ Do you mediate? Yoga?

"DO NOT ALLOW YOUR LONELINESS TO LOWER YOUR STANDARDS."
—UNKNOWN

FIND THE GOOD

Let's face it, co-parenting with a high-conflict person is excruciatingly challenging. In a matter of 60 seconds I'm sure you could rattle off at least 25 things that are awful in your co-parenting relationship right now.
Okay, maybe closer to 100.

I can't argue with you. Without a shadow of a doubt, I know your co-parenting situation is horrific or you wouldn't be reading this survival guide. I know you're scared to sleep at night, scared to wake up in the morning, scared about how your children will end up, scared about finances, scared about the future. You're scared. Almost all of the time.

I know you're angry. So angry that you clench your teeth to keep from screaming, your hair is falling out from stress, you have dark circles under your eyes, you have a short fuse and have crows-feet between your eyes from frowning.

I know you're at the end of your rope, you feel like giving up, you are drowning under the pressure of your co-parents demands, your body aches from the anguish you can't shake and you're lonely. So lonely.

I know you feel all alone, like no one understands or cares. I know you walk on egg shells. I know you are utterly and completely done with feeling like this. You just don't know how to make it all stop. You don't know what to do because you've tried everything and nothing has worked.

I also know there is only one way out of this hell you are living. One way out of the torture you are putting yourself through.

One way out of no longer thinking that if you could just fix a, b or c then maybe, just maybe, the conflict will dissipate.

> *Find the good.*
> In yourself first.
> Then others.
> *Find the good.*
> In the small things.
> Then in the bigger things.
> *Find the good.*
> Slowly if you need to.

It may seem too simple. It may seem great in theory but impossible in practice. It may seem like you just wasted a year moving your feelings to be told to Find the good.

But when you've been through what you've been through? Finding the good is not easy; in fact, it's very, very hard at times.

Find the good in yourself is:

- your way out of the mental, physical and emotional manipulative control your co-parent has over you
- your way into your own personal power
- is your secret to self-acceptance without judgement
- your freedom

Find the good.

> # "WEAK PEOPLE REVENGE. STRONG PEOPLE FORGIVE. INTELLIGENT PEOPLE IGNORE."
>
> —UNKNOWN

FEELINGS TO MOVE

- ☐ Grief
- ☐ Anger
- ☐ Over-excited
- ☐ Worry
- ☐ Fear

QUESTIONS

1. How can you *find the good* in your current co-parenting situation?
2. How can you teach your kids to *find the good?*
3. What does *find the good* feel like to you?

CHALLENGE

This week we challenge you to write a list of 10 areas in your life you can explore to Find the Good. If your kids are old enough, ask them to do the same.

TAKE CARE CHECKLIST

- ☐ How much sleep are you getting?
- ☐ How often do you get into nature?
- ☐ Have you taken a bath, Jacuzzi or sauna?
- ☐ Have you completed the Trigger Challenge?
- ☐ Are you spending time with friends?
- ☐ When was the last time you read a book for pleasure?
- ☐ Have you taken a walk recently?
- ☐ How often do you move your body?
- ☐ Are you eating well?
- ☐ Do you mediate? Yoga?

WELLNESS ASSESSMENT

KNOWING WHERE YOU ARE TODAY WILL HELP YOU KNOW WHAT TO SHOOT FOR IN YOUR SURVIVAL JOURNEY.

USING THIS SCALE, RATE THE FOLLOWING AREAS IN TERMS OF FREQUENCY

5   Frequently

4   Occasionally

3   Rarely

2   Never

1   It never occurred to me

PSYCHOLOGICAL WELLNESS

Write in a journal	
Go to a therapist	
Read books unrelated to work	
Take time to self-reflect	
Intentionally decrease stress in your life	
Track your emotions	
Let someone else be in charge	

SPIRITUAL WELLNESS

Have a spiritual community	
Spend time outdoors	
Be aware of nonmaterial aspects of life	
Pray	
Sing	
Volunteer to teach Sunday School or work with youth	
Read inspirational literature (talks, music, etc.)	

EMOTIONAL WELLNESS

Spend time with people you feel comfortable around	
Stay in touch with important people in your life	
Give yourself affirmations, praise yourself, love yourself	
Get out of the house	
Re-read favorite books, re-view favorite movies	
Allow yourself to cry	
Find things that make you laugh	

THIS WELLNESS ASSESSMENT WILL GIVE YOU A CLEAR PICTURE OF HOW WELL YOU ARE TAKING CARE OF YOURSELF AND AREAS WHERE YOU NEED TO IMPROVE. AFTER TAKING THIS BRIEF ASSESSMENT, YOU WILL BE READY TO DIVE INTO WEEK 1.

PHYSICAL WELLNESS

Eat nutritious foods and have a consistent eating schedule
Exercise (hike, dance, swim, walk, run, play sports, yoga)
Get regular preventive medical care and get medical care when needed
Get consistent sleep
Take time off when needed (vacations, weekend trips)
Get massages, pedicures, manicures
Take a day per week away from technology

INSIGHT WELLNESS

Allow others to know different sides or aspects of you
Notice your inner experiences like processing and listening to your attitudes, beliefs, feelings, thoughts
Do something new like going camping, to a museum, fishing, sporting events, auction, theater, etc.
Allow others to help you
Be curious
Say "no" on occasion when asked to help

WORK WELLNESS

Take breaks during the workday
Take time to chat with co-workers
Recognize when you are working too many hours
Recognize when you are taking on too much
Set limits with co-workers, customers, clients
Arrange your work space so it's comfortable/comforting

RESOURCES

CONFLICT PLAYBOOK

ConflictPlaybook.com/coparenting

ANDREA'S WEBSITE

AndreaLaRochelle.com

NEW WAYS FOR FAMILIES® ONLINE COPARENTING COURSE

NewWays4Families.com/pwc

NEW WAYS FOR FAMILIES® ONLINE COURSE FOR PARENTS AND KIDS

NewWays4Families.com/pcc

HIGH CONFLICT INSTITUTE

HighConflictInstitute.com

UNHOOKED BOOKS

UnhookedBooks.com

BIFF RESPONSES FOR WRITING TO DIFFICULT CO-PARENT

BiffResponse.com

ABOUT THE AUTHORS

ANDREA LAROCHELLE, RFM

is a registered mediator with over fifteen years' experience helping families through the challenges of separation and divorce. She is a trainer and speaker with the High Conflict Institute and serves on the board of the Alberta Family Mediation Society. She specializes in showing parents how to improve co-parenting communication and manage conflict more effectively, so their kids can focus on being kids. Andrea lives in Calgary, Alberta with her husband, children, and a few furry friends. Andrea's website is andrealarochelle.com

MEGAN HUNTER, MBA

is CEO of the High Conflict Institute in San Diego, California, which she co-founded with Bill Eddy, LCSW, Esq., who developed the high-conflict personality theory. She gives keynote speeches on conflict communication and provides training on high-conflict disputes to professionals around the world. She specializes in helping professionals learn skills to deal with challenging clients and co-workers. Previously, she was the Family Law Specialist at the Arizona Supreme Court, Administrative Office of the Courts. Megan and her husband, Paul, live in Scottsdale, Arizona.

OTHER BOOKS BY ANDREA

- *I'm Done! Take Control of Your High-conflict Divorce*
- *Goodbye Angry Bugs*
- *Goodbye Teary Bugs*
- *Goodbye Worry Bugs*

OTHER BOOKS BY MEGAN

- *Bait & Switch: Saving Your Relationship After Incredible Romance Turns Into Exhausting Chaos*
- *Dating Radar: Why Your Brain Says Yes to "The One" Who Will Make Your Life Hell*

CPSIA information can be obtained
at www.ICGtesting.com
Printed in the USA
LVHW050214260819
628792LV00002B/2/P